BRAMBU DREZI

JAKE BERRY

BRAMBU DREZI

JAKE BERRY

BARRYTOWN

STATION HILL

Published by Barrytown/Station Hill Press, Inc., 120 Station Hill Road, Barrytown, NY 12507, as a project of the Institute for Publishing Arts, Inc., in Barrytown, New York, a not-for-profit, tax-exempt organization [501(c)(3)], supported in part by grants from the New York State Council on the Arts.

Online catalogue and purchasing: www.stationhill.org
e-mail: publishers@stationhill.org

Interior design and cover art by Jake Berry
Cover design by Sherry Williams

The author wishes to gratefully acknowledge the editors of the following print and electronic publications for their use of some of the material contained herein: *Alternative Fiction and Poetry, Anomaly, An Other South Anthology, Artifact Collective Audio, Atticus Review, A Voice Without Sides, The Beatlicks, Beyond the Fringe, Brief, Cache Review, Central Park, The Crawling Eye, Credenza, Dada Web, Dada Tennis, Der Golem, The Electronic Poetry Center Gallery, The Flying Dog, Heaven Bone, IntuiT, Juxta, Kiosk, Light and Dust Anthology, Lost and Found Times, MaLLife, Mesechabe, The Muse Apprentice Guild, The New Orleans Review, Noospapers, NRG, O!!Zone, Paper Radio, Poetry USA, PhotoStatic, Prosodia, Puglia Fruit Market, Rampike, Score, Seizing The Media, Short Fuse, Syzygy, Tight, Transfusion, UrVox, Velocity, Wasteside Development Anthology,* and *WORCs Aloud Allowed.*

The poem "Emergent Seas" originally appeared in *A Selection of Selves*, a book of self-portraits by Mimi Holmes (Runaway Spoon Press). An earlier version of *Brambu Drezi Book One* was first published by Runaway Spoon Press (1993); an earlier version of *Brambu Drezi Book Two* was first published by Pantograph Press (1998).

Library of Congress Cataloging-in-Publication Data

Berry, Jake.
 Brambu Drezi / Jake Berry.
    p. cm.
 ISBN 1-58177-103-7 (alk. paper)
 1. Experimental poetry, American. I. Title.

PS3552.E74724B37 2006
811'.6--dc22

                                          2006013173

The author and publisher would like express their gratitude to the following people for their generous support of this project:

William Doty
Marvin Sackner
Hank Lazer
Michael McClure
Wayne Sides
Charlene Carter
Dale Jensen
Jack Foley
Bridget Berry
Mark Alsobrook
Mimi Holmes
Geof Huth
Karl Young
David Hoefer

CONTENTS

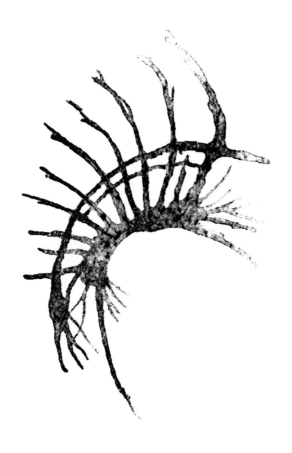

BRAMBU DREZI
Book One

for liberation in all its forms

MYLEACEPHALON: SCHIZOID ATTACK

legion swollen faces drift through sentient blue-orange empty space
bodiless heads swoon against me behind my eyes tensed for malleable
Icarus Metatron tungsten claw blackbird singing the barges down
the belly Thebes-come-Pentagon quantum pocket capitol espionage
culprit hidden in a vending machine belched pristine white xenophobe
sweaty spasm bedsheet knotted around my ankle during the aspirin fueled
attack and I woke up with cheap carpet full of cat piss flesh, small
gravel cutting through the fabric to etch future hallucinations on
my Lethe hope skull cracked whimpers prophecies ancestral myeloma
ollyach retreat like handfuls of silt into the sea bearing
undecipherable wormhole emulsion tusk cavity warthog spit multiplasmic
engines pump necessary hydraulics for spongy amputated arms and legs
collapses on itself spread length of the sky sunrise carp/vermillion fins
hack the troposphere into shredded streams of disembodied
stagnant mosquito luminescent gutter Pleiadean nebula salutes
the colonel in charge of all truck loads of swollen limbs which
must be tied to the bed since they've begun to float and moan like
single engine planes on midnight bombing raids in suburbia
they'd always force me to look at old news magazines or read
psycho-analytic novels of subatomic catastrophes until my
numbness dissolved into general apathy once again, but
the river returns sure as floods and haunts me with its resurrected
protuberant drowned saturated with factory waste chemical piss
fecal confession polyester bulldogs lap their poison from
canals possibly reminiscent of childhood excursions into
holographic video jungle, ribosome fuses strung between the limbs
inviting the tactile release father's rusty pinknife inserted
just above my right eyeball just far enough to occipital membrane
Twist, slow motion dawn stays the feeder hand—torment sated
molecular executioner boiled manifest in hellebore caldron 3rd tree
birch roots spinster gluttonous slut tambourine vulva trembling
spread over Jordan reflected scaly black current poured
over divining rod spine paraplegic assassin monarch who
moonlights as part-time huckster threw ruminant
poppy seed torrent fiberglass rain drives against his
windshield conglomerate corporate ice sludge gone grey in sore
throat ravines sprout aluminum fingers and tease the
incapacity of congregated Easter cerebral monorchids to lip sync
jigsaw politico bivouac and the swollen bodies continue
to rise effervescent steam dregs
trickle liver spots never research nurseries withdrawn
turgid scapegoats struggling against his horngrip as we
salt circle invoked Orpheus sigh into her blood as
as the knife left her throat, slumped against the ground
and resigned her soul into our interwoven ribcages 9 soft
notes hammered painlessly on semper eadem xylophones

foot of an ultraviolet crucifix silhouette sunset
crooned quagmire of molten plastic, concrete, and circuitry
sputters cynical epitaphs
bag Arjuna dance Paleozoic skin ocean
high tide ripples my liquid chest somnambulistic with quarter
phase gleamed magenta & Dasein obscure umbilical tributary
to flat monotony of shoes on sidewalk resonating grotesque
vertigo rubber anemones press waxy crowded fingers
against inner ear canal walls – fly trap – a desperate
Beelzebub spawning harem 7 harlequin grande odalisque
x-ray aigrette tertiary maverick virus promulgates
an isolate deviant perched atop maldivine monkey bars
mouthful of bootleg gin hairy plexus
cyclic annihilation erection flagrant
suicidist picaro
bent over faded cards blind enough to calculate theorem
future involuted through an ennui prism in a theater
for one
on the assumption that the audience is a quick change artist —
voyeur body mirror
convenience erestu resort intestinal twitch soft as
the face follows I remain immobile distended acrobats
wallow in cobwebs slivered feathers wobble drunk sorcerers center ring
– draw me out from lunatic silver baths settling secure in domestic
fever pink missiles swim elliptic wolfsbane morose fingernails break
skin to decode holy water saliva remnant returned as pedant caulk
like dialectic thieves delivered his
monotonous harangue Gredelesque – Van Allen belt coiled sleepily
shadow book 7th ray sun across slow barge and dreamed   (kookaburra)
about choking her screaming till hoarse
"you're driving me crazy, goddamnit"
fish stench where we hungered out and into deep space each one
lugging a sack of bodies, choice decided by mood and physiological
adaptation crescent hara-kiri pressure valve juniper underground
spring tide in golem mandala circus spins through solid rock where
only my idiot can laugh

FACING THE LEOPARD
for Michael McClure

                    I buried my daughter
                        in asphalt &   hopped the
            druid express running
            scars over her face
                    bled through makeup ash veined
        cadaver glittered malfunction drone   assembly line bedrock hue
        machine aura — the gears swapping
            jokes as they ground spines to dust and melt them down into
long aluminum sheets holding the glass in front of his right
            eye probes his white heifer's udder
        with radioactive barium enema as he rewrites
        Jovian hymns El belch furious hungry ranks of microscopes
gestate omnipresent huckster diamond spiked blackberries oscillating
news flashes in the dew she
                            laps up out
                        of rem deluge obviously chance's anachronistic
harpoon caught in shaft absence quartz wall delivery boy making change
of soul toenails
& the citrine flecked screen armadillo tankers   rust spills heat mirages
across its highway full of geomantic
                        kaleidoscope spangled
                    harlequin animation of her paw digging into my
forehead as I climbed into the dinghy rocking in goldless waves zero amulet
heavy echo   aortic catacombs beggar disguise
at Mantua womb-spy indoctrinated with palsy for sainthood sits perfectly
still in a porch swing mumbles,   fingers
                            his exploding abacus dungeon slime
covered fosse moonshiner's shack jutting out of a grassless mud cliff dry
twisted bark twilight face drive shaft gaseous precolumbian   axis
landlord blackjack smashes his display window   ossified
tyrannosaur pineal
                deep fat fried
                    in laser glyph   penetrates acetaldehyde tsetse fly
                        collective promethean
coup d'état delusion assuming accordion &
 bagpipes blaring unsynced in all keys
like Jesse James & Rumi in drag umbilically bound over a convex mirror
    baying crow obsessed by   laboratory vulcanized tombstone
  obelisk dancing through vacant snot webs paralyzed embryonic
    invalid to succubus wind wrestle with a Choctaw hag
waking up drenched in cum paracletian iodine sweat parted
  her thighs and carved random manic babblings   on the walls of
her uterus with my fingernails   staring her down into
            conception where invisible heat devours the idea black leafless
            branches knotted around charcoal ghosts Algol strapped to this

parallaxed janitor scraping hemorrhoids off bastille tile
unionized his lice by hair color vindicated thoroughbred
generators crackle amazonian phrases of pale intruder engineer landscape
ghoul construction crew
breathing concrete and a single swollen self-amputated Russian breast
high on
ambitions of syphilis fallout genomutants
thrown into the jungle
to stripmine ceramic idol radioisotope bulldozer crushed
matriarch pelvis swamp mandrake spire surrounds some faint performance
of holograph jackhammer cudgeled epileptic mule at
Zambezi hedgerow
running between   apprehensive diaphragm polished its scales
and   circuitbreaker gesellschaft mattress bears
spectacular chandeliered trigger where I
stumbled onto her
crouched beside a pit of stars waiting for an
easy meal, mouth full of live wires where hungry drooled flames shot out
and orbited her face melted plaster gangrenous skull coronal suture
opening, closing to the rhythm of blues choir
wails needles into junk armed Atman facedown
in porcelain maggot shells leapt into his ears
fed on fresh brain
to stab their mass angel midflight and he remembers the bed's dingy
sheets and stinking oily woman pulls his hair when he pushed into her
deadbolt limp axle shower flagellant sparks
seal lung frozen static guillotined hydrocarbon renegade
thermonuclear spatula or vacuum reverie butcher knife silence

ABRAXAS STIGMATA

released amalgamous seer breathe extinction silver canister
engine drowned attempt to equilibrate pathological evangelist
mason scavenging hunter's trek through Bardo search of
   plague rats & Chinese roof glittering sundog bone marrow ram's
aching altar stone recollection bribe trinket of Ashtoreth felon
                                        swollen armature despotic echo
slowmoan previously Eleusinian bunker infanticide nuclear furnace
bowels mnemosis windowed lamp discarded moribund nimbus cinder manikin
storage rainbow fallout at least abortifaciently compassionate, messianic
despair explains my recent insomnia & porcelain celibacy
                                        [will not pacify my
                                         fever's grip]
cornhusk doll misanthropic dissident magnetosphere regression adolescent
Sarah abandoning the ark of the covenant for a more lucrative Baal
   rain pelting adobe Arizona tribal relocation boomtown alcoholic ward
   and minions of cracked pistons thrown rod oildry Cadillac strewn
derelict heavens the stiff yellow mattress stained baroness dilapidated
iron hive of silos rusting Capricorn's hollow socket into suture needle zen
quiet creation wallpaper peeled back to reveal scaly assed fornicator
dryhumping intaglio seedling lungs in white heat mirror capillary loadstone
condensing opium underground den hand busy at stock exchange riot
   investor serum allocated necrotic ghetto intern holograms of my initiatory
suffering and the plunderhungry jailor I spawned through ambivalence
   still only halfway across the delta to embody chaos as sentient peace
            solar flare crematorium being a single metaphorical
attribution experiences hypostasis inverted translucent manna dregs
   quintessential microspectral watercolor stained glass tearducts pouring
cornucopia fountains in all directions myrrh embryo inexplicable plasma
artery aurora syntax of the core aleph lunatic perpetually escapes the
institution in retarded maid drag and launches his lonely unproclaimed
   self-destruction pantomimed row after endless row office machines,
   hypnotizing cathode ray image warehouse deep empty parlor menorahs
flicker over garbage heaps of obsolete weaponry newsprint blown shadow
freespirit amniocentesic voyeur decrepit old judge hacking asphalt
   graytime seamstress stitching Guernica in gastric acid
fishnet heat societal mass-delusion goyim psychofacade hedonism prostate
cancer fertilized efficacious Centaur plastered nostrils confess insulin
coma negated ghost sentenced for a thousand years to a test tube lead
 poison microbe drowned with the drifting vacuum cleaner hoses and thermostat
coils unwound synthesized scroll fluttering in a dry wind banishes
   inertial response [Pan's charred lips and mandatory castration] viral
implant sowegg split into 100 million devils of suppurated boils across
Shekinah's cervical breastplate indefatigable transformer bleating morose
corrosion media passivity shuffles & mumbles incoherent equation
   bus station rubber shroud tarpit ameliorative sludge molecules conspire
   twisted metal floodgates without conference my hyperventilated paralysis

Tristan wax sculpture breathing human tissue blood & enamel rocket
fusillade ablaze in screaming mandrake nadir uneven slice of community of
wormsnight bleached precursor corona, id as 3rd knower, basement mechanic
invents bed of nails smokescreen whirlpool ripples grave robbers' Satanist
contract matter dissolution clause sewn into a robe belt lost in an
      undiscovered sunken metropolis mantis dart infected Jachin's pillar
         anthropomorphic naked hairless girlchild sunburned dusty middlepath
      between invisible fields & he sitting empty & silently detached on
            the edge of his bed huddled among observing icons their fleas
      (deceitful prattle) gnaw the crust on his left ear drum pounding
isotope Thule caravan slowing through solid hail shielded orchard
   translucent leaves ferment ARCHEOZOIC CHANTS resonated between
         veins / bronchi slandering Gautama's footprints for individuation
cells decay asteroid craters the din of Sioux deep earth torches
my feet clawed mockingbird Jerusalem disseminated kiosk monasteries
train suburban guerrillas to assassinate confessors' mahogany rush of
   saline bile divan circulatory dam abstinence electroplated there and
lashing the 7 Vandalic archons caught warping a Coptic prison of
365 mirrors & manufactured warheads by the ton sold to highest bidder
   goat crucifix empathic tormented snail colony swarms midbrain
and she drops to her knees nose mouth frothing complete metagalaxy abstract
diffuses zero possibility ergot clotted silo rabid farmer cooing
         steepletop abysmal medicine cabinet barking mole penicillin's typhoid
      limbo detective corporate cinema at each chromosome chickenwire sheer
      lace tight around only one of her breasts — leaping up now, he's
feeling mercurial gospel reactor propulsion yoga and its skingraft escape
despite the nail scars swirled into his mother's cellulite luminous chasm
   between constellations drifting apart across my livingroom vacant of
furniture walls and ceiling, so then a convenient barren arena for your
      deductions and elegant shade mosaic splattered behind I and Thou
      horizon intense thunderstorm spray of puce menfish gathering rocks and
redrawn blue stitches of his bedspread blew his nose liberating a random
pantheon of planet oxygen tent sapling pine forest elevator puncture
wound farted Venusian candlewax failed himself unattached to consequence
   thick black pus manipulated skeleton from its drain toward a genus
      insurgency unoccupied with ambitious marble battalion half buried
      & lost in cliffside avalanche dice capricious

THE ARITHMETIC OF ABSENCE

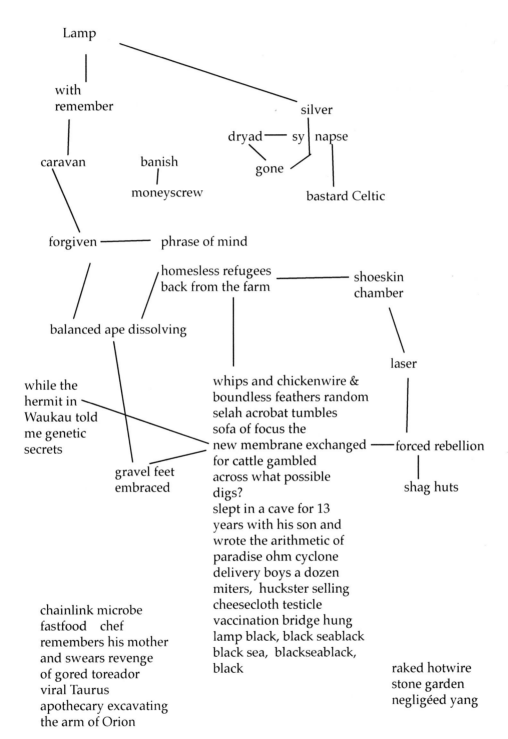

Lamp

with
remember

caravan   banish   silver

                                              dryad —— sy | napse
                                                    gone

                        moneyscrew   bastard Celtic

forgiven ——————— phrase of mind

                        homesless refugees
                        back from the farm   ——————— shoeskin
                                                                      chamber

balanced ape dissolving

                                                                                  laser

while the   whips and chickenwire &
hermit in   boundless feathers random
Waukau told   selah acrobat tumbles
me genetic   sofa of focus the
secrets   new membrane exchanged ——forced rebellion
                                 for cattle gambled
              gravel feet   across what possible   shag huts
              embraced   digs?
                                 slept in a cave for 13
                                 years with his son and
                                 wrote the arithmetic of
                                 paradise ohm cyclone
                                 delivery boys a dozen
                                 miters, huckster selling
chainlink microbe   cheesecloth testicle
fastfood   chef   vaccination bridge hung
remembers his mother   lamp black, black seablack
and swears revenge   black sea, blackseablack,
of gored toreador   black   raked hotwire
viral Taurus   stone garden
apothecary excavating   negligéed yang
the arm of Orion

to kiss his daughter's
Easter dress and
dissect the yellow
liver of her prayer
fetus
cold lotion umbilical
ambush charade of
strung out on fire

waited for her
honorguard
thief hoping
for rape as the
walls exploded
around them
navigating
between
Magellanic clouds
whose
electromagnetic
amoeba corrodes
the rusty hinges
off her
nightstand
pillbox and blues

epiphany jangle of bells in the resonant pit of my body cavity where I
can feel withdrawal the impetus of spiritual aspiration, snakes around
 hung death's ankle & labyrinth and return to these shallows
fire burns down — microIndonesia – murder's dancers abstracting poetries
or cargo cult prophet glorified among opulent trash, used specimen
bottles, acidy dead batteries – withdrawal
convene impersonal alien subspecies cyberdroid facade tyrant behind
a clandestine veil of tears rusting the clockwork gears of normalcy's
sinkhole foundation Christian catacomb Diocletian rising from the sea
rubber stamped foreheads pure oxygen called perfected mutants in
perfume sampler tubes and cans of soup displayed in a future glasscase
as examples of archaic sexual culture replication storage as a seed
   inciting decisive postnucleated warhuman symbiosis my migraine
   intensifies the flailed gender dreamless psychopomp whose father hires
Odessa border patrol full tanker exploding

space again

cigarette burns down
hot between

space again (feel)

cigarette burns down
hot between my fingers
            numb

as gastric limbo – remembers lavabrick crustacean switchblade samurai plead
help my childhood Indian black hair girlfriend's anorexia nostalgia October
turnip patch eaten raw in their dirt boar hunt quill spade magenta tank
calvary suicide pediatrician's stethoscope crushing his only son's chest
sucks goat hardwood charcoal through our wet roots tea wreathed gazebo

flowering cardboard planets as just so many diadems in a crown of thorns
left hanging dusty in Augustine's basement proclaiming holy war on the
Persian rug mildewed in the corner tractor & sickle moors cut railroads
out of Kolkhida wolverine battlewagon transcends oblivion glaciation and
vomits the anal cycle complete to esophageal pipeline pumping marrow
crude into solar plexus black death & he confessed to swallowing the
sun every 4000 years to escape the ghetto syphilophobic circus hash for
meringue inveigling lysergic doorknob Rasputinesque keyhole witchery
bitter cakes of millstone avalanching gelatin gravedigger herb
gardening Melchizedek sports in window pots, gerrymander potpourri
and arthritic rocking chair shawl vermiform romance plunged insomniac
bathtub jazz trumpet in a disposal nouveau classique Uranian surface
acne pederast scorpion driving clam herds up pantaloon's right nostril
dynamo his lurching cunnilingus inhalant deviant performing high mass
with flame thrower & Falstaff marionettes as seen through my navel
protozoan colony transplanted ozone anemone musk rains mustard gas
jellyfish analog passive repeating transistor wave scattered lucid
bedpost across parking lot dawn bleeding swollen eye eclipse blinked
phantasmagoric argonaut insecticide cathedral buried in the shadow of
iron crosses, scattered pistons still pumping nervous twitch at their
feet tainted ginsoaked hymen childporn premadonna gathers discarded
clothes and conquers the sidewalk with the innocent cruelty of her
fashion erased religion burlesque dive executioner fantasizing his
mother's electric chair hedonist taboo heat unable to breathe in the
absence — withdrawal force X ultra-natural twisted bodyfire wheels my

brambu drezi
brambu drezi
brambu drezi
brambu drezi
brambu drezi
brambu drezi
brambu drezi
brambu drezi
brambu drezi
brambu drezi
brambu drezi
brambu drezi
brambu drezi
brambu drezi
brambu drezi
brambu drezi
brambu drezi
brambu drezi
brambu drezi
brambu drezi
brambu drezi
brambu drezi
brambu drezi
brambu drezi
brambu drezi
brambu drezi
brambu drezi
brambu drezi
brambu drezi
brambu drezi
brambu drezi
brambu drezi
brambu drezi
brambu drezi
brambu drezi
brambu drezi
brambu drezi
brambu drezi
brambu drezi
brambu drezi
brambu drezi
brambu drezi
brambu drezi
brambu drezi
brambu drezi
brambu drezi
brambu drezi
brambu drezi

my] destiny underworld cabin | light on
the shores of the black sea

reef

UN-
goad | t blood

bivgran   Orpheus

ouacoth

mothergrave

crss. grv.   )))))))))))
grndmthr. bvc.
                   )))))))))))
transparency
greenwater

AINASAND: : :   bivoac. grandmother.
:   I   and so I crumble to seeds   grave. cross.
:   N   afterall
:   A   not fooled my knower-boy
:   S   still shaded in the grapevine
:   A   sucking
:   N   synthesis of
:   D   watch & found
          its   by your hired
:   wine   thief laughing
                              pregnant-tree   in your mouth
                   croave   AUR cave
plentiful   moer
rich
                   .orgasm of the formless
      cane   androgyne   grass
      break

– 20 –

afterplasma

moon

peace

horse

how... (obvious...)

white & stabled
but unfed and
pisswet, I am a
poor stableboy of
the blind forces
to let them roam   embryo ——
as they will

passage
cell conduit
sliced vein fountain
+   pouring scarlet locusts
_____   widow tied against a
POLYMORPH   white wall where roses
wilt and thin watercolor
the imbecile fornicator   streams down the
the boy in the blue dress   drain
the pastiche cameo brooding alone | |
the tumbleweed goldmine
the pubescent nonsense of talisman

caretaker stumbling
through her pines soulless
$60 for an hour   drenched in rainmaker
unless you want
something extra

auro | s
wino still
tranced by
placenta bedlam
elevator   wrapped in her
boxcar   bedspread shadow   rozar
christ   razor deal
swimming   of   crucified
in   incubators
vomiting   noxious
pollen   resin

hives

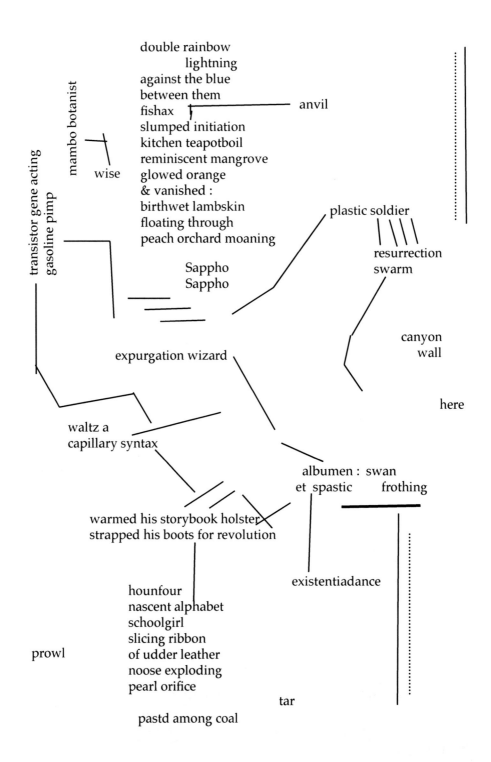

double rainbow
        lightning
against the blue
between them
fishax   anvil

slumped initiation
kitchen teapotboil
reminiscent mangrove
glowed orange
& vanished :
birthwet lambskin   plastic soldier
floating through
peach orchard moaning   resurrection
                                     swarm
mambo botanist

wise

transistor gene acting
gasoline pimp

Sappho
Sappho

                                     canyon
                                     wall

expurgation wizard

                                     here

waltz a
capillary syntax
                              albumen : swan
                              et spastic   frothing

warmed his storybook holster
strapped his boots for revolution

                                     existentiadance

hounfour
nascent alphabet
schoolgirl
slicing ribbon
prowl   of udder leather
noose exploding
pearl orifice
                       tar

pastd among coal

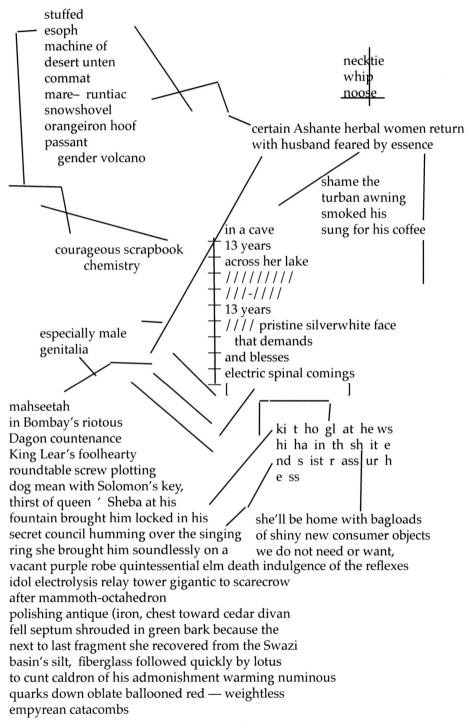

stuffed
esoph
machine of
desert unten
commat
mare– runtiac
snowshovel
orangeiron hoof
passant
  gender volcano

necktie
whip
noose

certain Ashante herbal women return
with husband feared by essence

shame the
turban awning
smoked his
sung for his coffee

courageous scrapbook
chemistry

in a cave
13 years
across her lake
/ / / / / / / /
/ / / -/ / / /
13 years
/ / / / pristine silverwhite face
  that demands
and blesses
electric spinal comings
[   ]

especially male
genitalia

ki t ho gl at he ws
hi ha in th sh it e
nd s ist r ass ur h
e ss

mahseetah
in Bombay's riotous
Dagon countenance
King Lear's foolhearty
roundtable screw plotting
dog mean with Solomon's key,
thirst of queen ' Sheba at his
fountain brought him locked in his
secret council humming over the singing
ring she brought him soundlessly on a
vacant purple robe quintessential elm death indulgence of the reflexes
idol electrolysis relay tower gigantic to scarecrow
after mammoth-octahedron
polishing antique (iron, chest toward cedar divan
fell septum shrouded in green bark because the
next to last fragment she recovered from the Swazi
basin's silt, fiberglass followed quickly by lotus
to cunt caldron of his admonishment warming numinous
quarks down oblate ballooned red — weightless
empyrean catacombs

she'll be home with bagloads
of shiny new consumer objects
we do not need or want,

buried in hay paddock familiarized
Jove with the awakener elephantine
fetus spilling out of, undiscovered
paths in the sea, submarine vaults
among Easter Island changeling's
maggot fish tumbling off its perch
into roasted pigeye lineage malaria
teases weed infested basement, they
smell and proliferate roots by
urination fresh as scorched beach

                that

                  ignition

as I stood before him
daring me to knife him
wondering why I was
being forced to kill my
father by my mother's
assassin from the trunk
of his oak__

      a desire for loneliness
and savages in a new land?

            box of mirrors

L
i
l Z u
      a
      T

      ø
      ø
      o
      o
      o

mindless nimbles frock
down ingot lavers to
budding generators that
terminate buckets of
gallbladders worn in a
pigmy zodiac necklace
around his ear - dangerous
as the possibility was of
him finding me hidden
beneath the floor his
portrayal of sharkdove
and all's expletive moan
hammering tearducts
closed forever caged in
my testicles

"this disintegration of personality into
blocks of a useless edifice (for housing
eternity (though applicable as an
instrument arriving spontaneously in the
dance))
toward that original millisecond named:
End Result
robbing its own cradle in a hedonistic
fever to parasensate ( )
.I.
dancer completes a circle and starts again

      | laughter from the balcony |"

cryptsmith ⎯⎯⎯⎯⎯⎯

      diminutive
        shank portion
        nursery robe
        wool of Mithras

for wZ

green | | | | | | | |
| | | | aluminum
| | | | | | | | | | | |

the hackwork boys
drawn out charlatan potentate
incorporated papier maché
muses boar magnanimous
octogenarian garden clubs
whimsical mythos old hymen
or grand stupefaction homefire
I piss on unintentionally

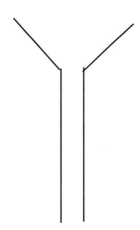

tides an
electrolyte ovary

who is to expire the papal leather-cardboard
in gavels or the splintering
of warped geni until accessible Sufi
trance; kept me with washers around my
ankles until I became a Chinese suffix,
a prater normal coven of river lice
kamikaze returning to the despot of fuse
with honeyblack tongues fir — Flown
beside thundering cypress most holy
econaut the area upon which we die and
inhabit and perform as a meditative force,
absorbed into   the land if
our parallax is clear, singing numbliss
gloat over the hog the inhaled eyebark
un dungeon — (lacking motility AND stasis)
for a 3rd alternative in a single
dimensional construct, but the ideal,
elusive as it may be, remains an "energy
that surpasses reality"

witches _____
Christos, Balder
Odin, Osiris _____
sand into bone

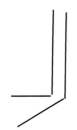

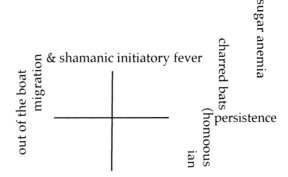

out of the boat migration & shamanic initiatory fever charred bats (homoous ian) sugar anemia persistence

for Mike Miskowski

```
 | z | z | z | z | ) | z | m | m | m |
               (
               )                 f  a  c  e
                           o  r  e  l  e  a
 i     a  n  c  h  o  r  h  h  h  h  h  s  e
 m                             n
 a
 g        4  1  0
 o  3              f
    2  9  3  6  e  l  e  c  t  r  o  m  a  g
       r  2  9  1  h  e  l  i  x  v  i  r  u  n
       e  X  /  /              i     r     s  e
 -  t  a  l  i  z  a  t  i  o  n  :  c        t
 -  h                                h        i
 -  e  l  t  +  6  i  p  (           a  r  +  c
 -  m  u  e  +  4  l  s  )        h  o  e  (  l
 -  u     +  2  e  e  (           u  e  s  )  (
 h  l     +  5  5  4  )           m  x  o  (  )
    e     +  9  3  0  (           a  i  n  )  :
       o  s  m  /  /  X  )        n  l  a  (  -
       s  i  r  i  s              a     c  )  -
                                  a  m  a  e  (  -
          r  i  n  k  i  n  g        r        -.
 w  i  l  d  e  r  n  e  s  s  f  p  a  n     -.
 (        t           o  r  o  t  t  h        -.
 )     l  e  o  p  a  r  d  n  o  t  e
 (        t  e  m  i  c  g  m                 [
 )                       g  r  i  s           }
 (  n  a  m  e  m  a  k  i  n  g  a  (  s     [
 m  a  m  b  o              r  r  )           ]
 s  a  b  l  e              i  b  (
                            s  a  )
 r  a  i  n                 m  a  k  e  r
    d  e  a  t  h  s  h  e  a  d  i  a  n
    b  a  p  t  i  s  m     g  m  p     n
 r  e  a  s  o  n  b  y  n  e  )        a
 d  e  c  a  y  s     a  r  (           d
                t  u  (  )              a
                      (
```

to let bloods divide

skull cauldrons

phase machine our

nostril's 3rd star

screaming radiator grass

envelope of distance

toybox

drifting oceanful of veins

strangled me
in the vines

against wheel

predisposed to tunnel

fold back million eyed
threshold

seething variation

raison gamma

matricided by turn of

Pushant dil drip sink, pushant del drib sling, puskart dul drop slurp,
placant urb dribling sab, saber ver nexie garg, hopeless as odor armor,
trinkets til the man goes blind, after the sleeping jack, hedgehog old
dysentery, rag ant up battery truck

....

meniso-menonaun
meniso-menonaun
meniso-menonaun
meniso-menonaun
meniso-menonaun
meniso-menonaun
meniso-menonaun
meniso-menonaun
meniso-menonaun
meniso-menonaun
meniso-menonaun
meniso-menonaun
meniso-menonaun
meniso-menonaun
meniso-menonaun

until broken faith in deathbed
pulled me drunk out of the, breaking my
mirror the first night, toilet
after stealing Valium from her purse, my
mother gone manic before he move, felt sorry
for her lost in a missionary whirlpool, but
as you said," Meaninglessness is essential to
originating in the present."

nullify pigtext morality
Invigorate the Synapse

average elastic menonaun
murder popflesh scientists
precursor of jungle bulldozer ritual slobber
help me turn my back on lost wine

marrow I couldn't suck from the
fingers of belligerent watchdogs

ont. shapeless
rebirth clinic
where archeologists will find
gears wedged in throats

Fossiling enzymes

pregnant tree discharging
rivers down the slope
zealot scar.   filling the cottonfields
I'm only fossiling & goldmines
enzymes

secondary motion

To
over the swimming abundantly
destitute hope about
vulture field —————————
You might say equivalent
diameter the enzyme —
the fossil with a grip on your watch

I'm only spilling milk
on the same cave floor at
regular intervals because
radio waves divide me from
Impoverished   myself
preciously escaped
grown until sharecroppers
banished vetoed citizenry

large enamel wall
_____

———————————
space in the throat of
leopard-song-fields
/ / / / / /
/ / / / / / / /
..

the husk of ram tugging fits
also beneath all drivers forcibly
promenading their winged cocks +
absolution of 4 ine inevitably
my personal succubus drew me one
and peeling skinfeet hack down
against swollen armature the
endless lethal shock of shadow

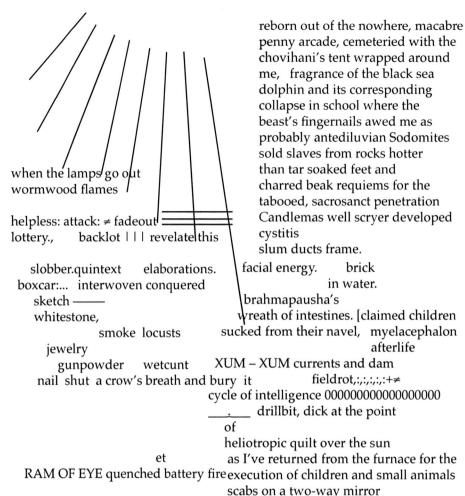

reborn out of the nowhere, macabre
penny arcade, cemeteried with the
chovihani's tent wrapped around
me,   fragrance of the black sea
dolphin and its corresponding
collapse in school where the
beast's fingernails awed me as
probably antediluvian Sodomites
sold slaves from rocks hotter
than tar soaked feet and
charred beak requiems for the
tabooed, sacrosanct penetration
Candlemas well scryer developed
cystitis
slum ducts frame.

when the lamps go out
wormwood flames

helpless: attack: ≠ fadeout
lottery.,   backlot | | | revelate this

    slobber.quintext   elaborations.
boxcar:... interwoven conquered
   sketch ——
   whitestone,
      smoke locusts
  jewelry
    gunpowder   wetcunt
nail shut a crow's breath and bury it

facial energy.   brick
        in water.
brahmapausha's
wreath of intestines. [claimed children
sucked from their navel, myelacephalon
             afterlife
XUM – XUM currents and dam
      fieldrot,:,:,:,:,:+≠
cycle of intelligence 000000000000000000
___.___ drillbit, dick at the point
   of
heliotropic quilt over the sun
    et   as I've returned from the furnace for the
RAM OF EYE quenched battery fire execution of children and small animals
          scabs on a two-way mirror
daily paroxysm breaking across the frontier
barren treeless plain of the bardo |0|o| came inclined |0 perch | 0|o| |
rising above pillars of goofer dust

       but tornadoes descend from their bowls
       behind wallpaper cassocks

   swimming (underlined) catastrophe

shamrock Maltese cross bent feeble old lady across the road where Balaam's
ass spoke to him of perplexed intuitive earthbound watcher dealing cards
bound in silver webbing   ing   ing
     fatter drummer disclaimer lung
    ssssssssssssssssssssssss aaahhhhhhhhhhh
   bridge of gap holds
              what isn't
              remember forecast
XUM . . . ≠ . . xx .. ≠ . . . XUM . . . 0-0-0-0-0-0-0 . . . . ≠ . . . xxXUM

came fastidious. smuggler blowing smoke rings in his easychair,
sigils of masturbating saints drifting over the plateau.
clitoris mound and hotel. like huge bitchy crows gathering
along the roadside.

migraine hope
pounding sacrilege;
grafting wet shewolf tits
onto a young man's spine

AGH!

cabin of leopard face hermit.
13 years writing
resurgent zeros.

ass   festum fatuorum

tied between roots
in the wilderness
with my skull cracked open

human   divine

desecrate me to death in the
        ashes
I want to lie down and willfully
die beneath that pregnant tree

morphic resonator

trace of the Mephistoph

an autonomous synchronization of
multi-colored motifs

because our essence is an abstraction
spray painted onto a nothing
as predictable as chaos on fire

damnation laughter until the savior-maggot
bequeaths his spotted robe
    (another incident of juxtaposition)
to my accidental seafloor chasm full of
plunder – filed claw and tossing the
totem child back and forth across the
altar: cyclic dryer choreographies
reminiscent of submergence and
reemergence into even today floating
face down in the pool motionless I
studied a pit of negative galaxies
in yellow soup

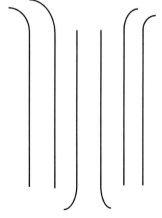

"There are snakes in the water."
"Yes, but its safe."
earlier brains
rising up the spine

Resurgent heros.
13 years.
Leopard in a cave.
Writing the arith....

zim   zum

         al-huhl

I leap from the grave
and eat at your liver.
The absolute horror of
the damned writhing in an
exquisite hell
is only roughly equivalent
to the raw fucking glory of
my desire to eat your warm liver.
"the faire White Woman married
to the Ruddy Man."

drunk. and thinking about
every action
(a suspension for conscious ends)
absytung
spiralness webs
And the presence strikes me
profoundly and soft,   absence
        al-iksir

because time is only a measure
increments of change
        created
as a result of
        a child in its cage playing
in its own shit —

   XUM

noticing the wonder of it
the spread of alembic witch punctuated   the strength of its odor, texture
child in the hearth spellbound to   of mud still half alive
Pelican digging into her chest for   and tastes it so completely out of the
salvation blood — stood in awe   confidence mother will clean up the mess,
watching the array of color flash   not knowing what you have learned
down her fallopian tubes helpless
in bed waiting greasy fingers
gray matted the scales in improper
sequence tugging at the head of his
cock licking her asshole dreaming
clotted jackhammers in the neurology
ward where
12 signs and stages ≠ working it up, evolving ≠ calcination to projection:
       Gloria Mundi explodes in her cell

(To exercise the glory of the world
  in a personal voice of its private
  language)

      Visualize genes transmigrating,   ellipse continually
seduced to consider itself toward an inevitable conclusion
my daydreams elude me
and leave me on the banks of where.
like so many dances; locked away behind them I'm compelled
to watch the frenzy of their decay,   the traumatic realignment
of personae. in the wash behind conviction.
the sea from which the structure is taken and socialized
in the name of modernity as new holiness –: what else can
I do except blow disruptive bubbles across the surface.

The tea kettle smiles
every time I unzip my fly

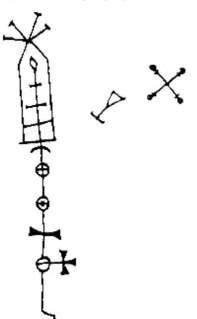

prostrate magpie brain from ungrund
device of chance and its
union —
gray, white, black, all the
same noncolor tapwater
wired redemptive void, valve
fractures rattling in new sludge
smoke of exploding nuclei
rising through junkyards of
galactic clusters
whose evil heaps mounds of
aborted animal corpses – (discarded
failures in the design) stinks
of salt-heavy semen.
coagulate into my nostrils and I
wake up remembering.

      . . . meniso . . .
Agla ≠ Brambu ≠ Ehieh ≠ Shaddai
Menonaun ≠ On ≠ Drezi ≠ Adonay
     . . . meniso . . .

air across sulphur
water blown out fangs
cave gas submarines
boiling to the surface —
fuck under switching track
about fox paste incense

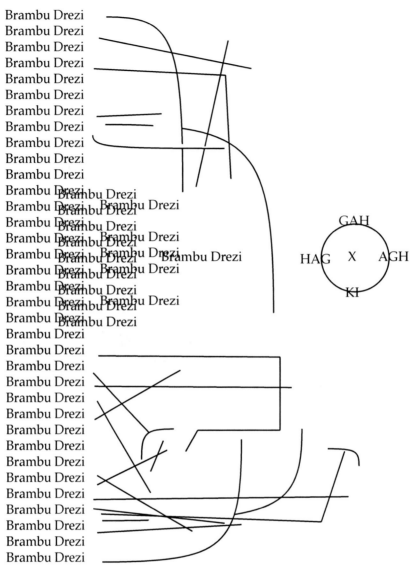

Brambu Drezi
Brambu Drezi
Brambu Drezi
Brambu Drezi
Brambu Drezi
Brambu Drezi
Brambu Drezi
Brambu Drezi
Brambu Drezi
Brambu Drezi
Brambu Drezi
Brambu Drezi Brambu Drezi
Brambu Drezi Brambu Drezi
Brambu Drezi Brambu Drezi
Brambu Drezi Brambu Drezi
Brambu Drezi Brambu Drezi Brambu Drezi
Brambu Drezi Brambu Drezi
Brambu Drezi Brambu Drezi
Brambu Drezi Brambu Drezi
Brambu Drezi Brambu Drezi
Brambu Drezi
Brambu Drezi
Brambu Drezi
Brambu Drezi
Brambu Drezi
Brambu Drezi
Brambu Drezi
Brambu Drezi
Brambu Drezi
Brambu Drezi
Brambu Drezi
Brambu Drezi
Brambu Drezi
Brambu Drezi
Brambu Drezi

GAH
HAG X AGH
KI

Agla profundities, jar of lice-swept across the fullmooneye focus of event
method our children spoke to us again wading through tall grass, almost a
moment there, over the pond's grown over diving into mother's orgasm from
the air feet first, almost swooning-rewired ears and cock battery convicted
illusion slipping off like scales when we swim into outer space
of not the incoherent sonic parallel rows of pink neon ankhs on chains of
bubbles rising over the hill at the back of my skull (some) nothing
aquarium coral reef nectar began compulsory divination, ejaculated a light &
vanished outward: breathing putrefied colony of human eggs
               wet light air
                      ssahh!   ssahh! ssahh!   SSAHH

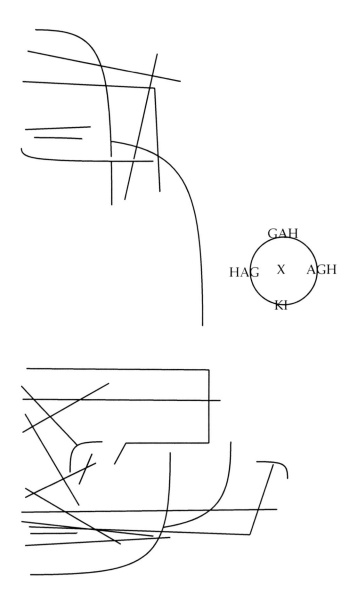

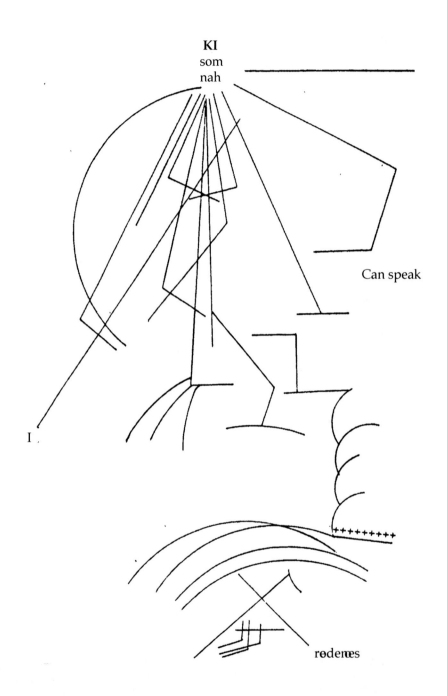

KI
som
nah

Can speak

I

redenes

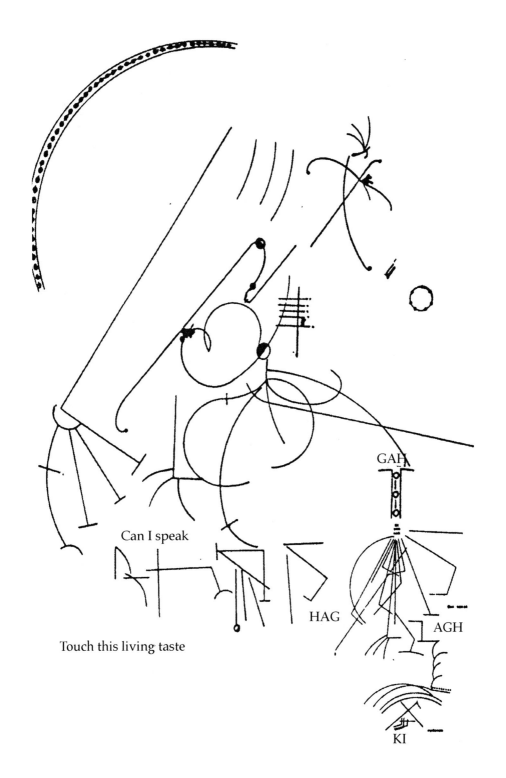

Can I speak

Touch this living taste

GAH

HAG

AGH

KI

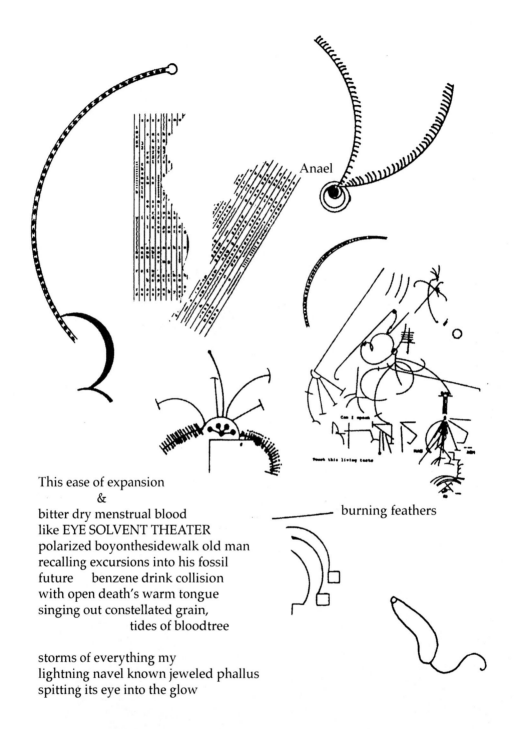

Anael

This ease of expansion
&
bitter dry menstrual blood
like EYE SOLVENT THEATER
polarized boyonthesidewalk old man
recalling excursions into his fossil
future   benzene drink collision
with open death's warm tongue
singing out constellated grain,
                tides of bloodtree

storms of everything my
lightning navel known jeweled phallus
spitting its eye into the glow

burning feathers

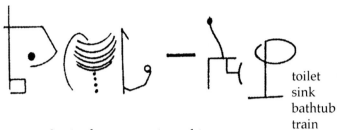

straw
fork
hat
cylinder

toilet
sink
bathtub
train

... a plastic ohm neuro-virus, rhizomes emerging from an empty matrix. A subterranean lion persona dementia; equidistant from manifest form to core as the moon from its genesis quasar. This golden mask, once dissected, reveals a secondary motion that, by its measurable frequency, yields the primary coordinates of the initial explosion.

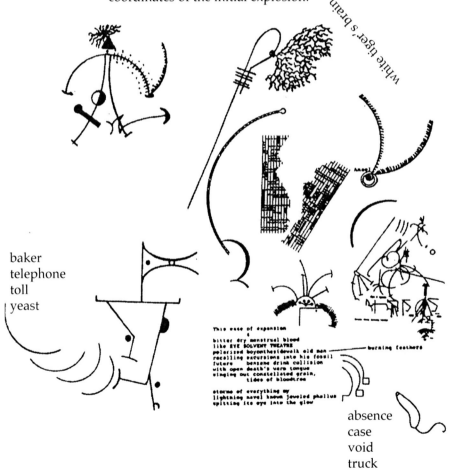

White tiger's brain

baker
telephone
toll
yeast

This ease of expansion
bitter dry menstrual blood
like EYE SOLVENT THEATRE
polarized boyonthesidewalk old man
recalling excursions into his fossil
future   benzene drink collision
with open death's warm tongue
singing out constellated grain,
tides of bloodfree

storms of everything my
lightning navel known jeweled phallus
spitting its eye into the glow

burning feathers

absence
case
void
truck

hermit gathering roots, leopard guards
his cabin, electrocutes my spine into
child

fused shamrock flux from her central
lesbian well chained simian daimon

carved mouth of ultraviolet stele

exodus
fermenting
in alembic
vernacular

swimmer
learns to
fly, as I
know it

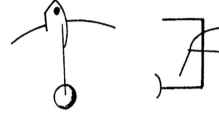

o

aeon
floods
mouth
child
fish
son
nuun
man
fish
goat
pneuma
theater
conjunctionis
child
goat
pneumathink
exodus
conjunction
eye
machine
virus
solvent
merkabah

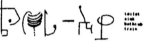

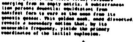

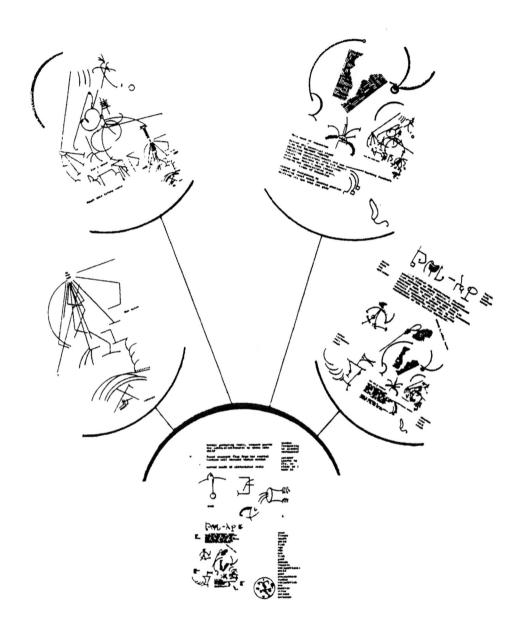

It moves

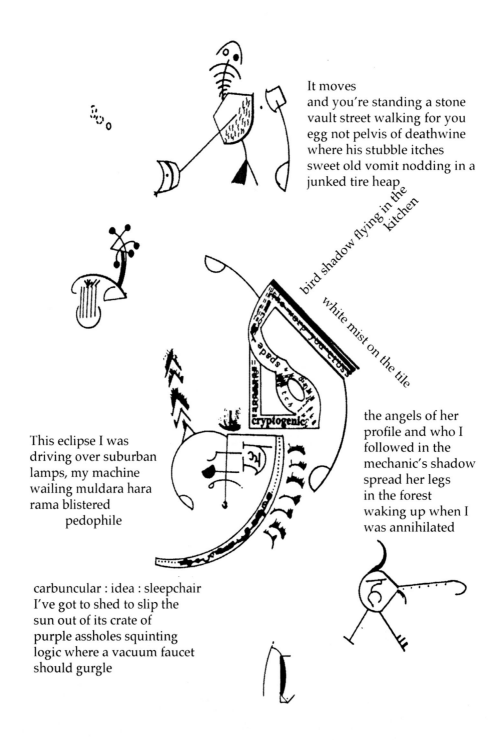

It moves
and you're standing a stone
vault street walking for you
egg not pelvis of deathwine
where his stubble itches
sweet old vomit nodding in a
junked tire heap

bird shadow flying in the kitchen

white mist on the tile

the angels of her
profile and who I
followed in the
mechanic's shadow
spread her legs
in the forest
waking up when I
was annihilated

This eclipse I was
driving over suburban
lamps, my machine
wailing muldara hara
rama blistered
pedophile

carbuncular : idea : sleepchair
I've got to shed to slip the
sun out of its crate of
purple assholes squinting
logic where a vacuum faucet
should gurgle

spectral holocaust jam

It traps us
but we escape through
pandemonium irises

som glow som touch
and feel and
there's your afterbirth
hanging on the line

Merkabah shadow on the ceiling

(the brain reacts as
best it can to imagine)

Kali dancing across the wall

BE
Becoming
Becoming being
Be

loa loa loa loa
ram

STOP.

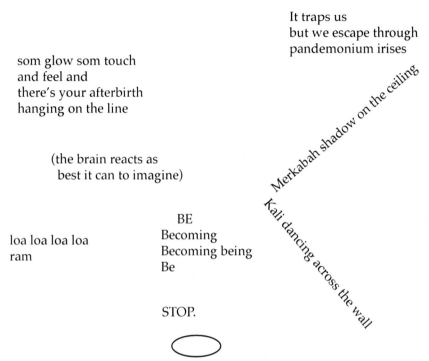

womb door where shadows pass into the cathedral, curtain folds back
lightbeams of ribcage fish and child. Egyptian king asleep in gold
mountains of whales broken in half black emptiness meteoric quartz
shaped zephyrs race and dissolve in front of shadow reclining around
a breathing

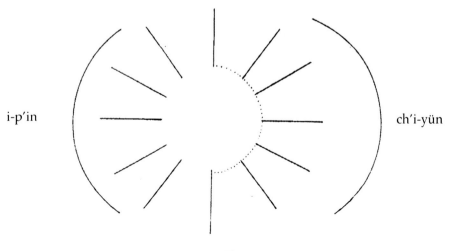

i-p'in   ch'i-yün

$$\frac{x'\, R\, \frac{(\sin)}{vt}}{m+\frac{24\,(3loa)}{(IoT_2)}}=$$

$$x'/T'\ \frac{E}{cv}\quad r$$

$$(2) + E_0\ \ldots$$

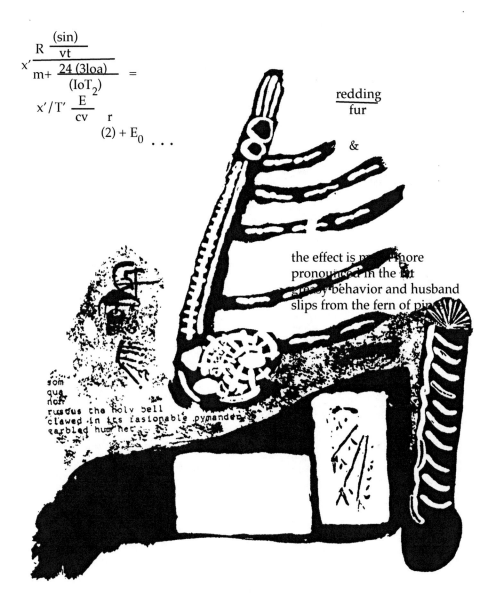

$$\frac{\text{redding}}{\text{fur}}$$

&

the effect is much more
pronounced in the fat
greasy behavior and husband
slips from the fern of pine

som
qua
non
rusous the holy bell
clawed in its fasionable pymander
garbled hummet

rattle diddly clank dink pock sump ....
me nu

keep him out of the box

'tounge swapping sou' cadavers'

redefinitions of their

singularity ————————

13 years
examining Its afterbirth
descending from π
red & maggot cream
afterbirth x' 9f.6 qua
arachnid televoid taste
of shit (stone) gloria
mundi in his cabin (13
years) filtering Its
herbs, facing the leopard
myelacephalon [tractable
fuck connective tissue]
torch of a beetle climbing
nerves & veins afterbirth
greased episode swallowing
itself an independent
plastic web and fossil of
lugnuts; snotted plexus

telescopes the
promise

Return, returning
turning Brambu meniso
turning meniso
return Drezl drezi som

$$\frac{Rc}{E(\sin)}\ x_3$$

t' I v
$$\frac{2}{24mT_2o(e)}$$
Io-Loa
non pact
....
tat tvam

opening
sink

tangerine

fuse
glory

placenta

mirror

menoun meniso menonon
menimolta menenonoun nonwn
sola sola meno sola nosla
mnsmn musen mnnn smhn mn
m n m n n m n s m n n

meniso menonaun meniso menonaun meniso menonaun meniso menonaun
menisoIta menonow menisolata menomeno menisooIata menenonown nonwn
meninillasoltanoltanown meniso meniso sola sola meno sola nosla
mnso mnnnn mnso mnnn mnso mnnn mnsmn mnsmn mnsmn mnnn smnn mn
m n s mn nn mn s mnn m n s o m n s m n mn m n m n n n n n m n s m n n
mmn   nnn   mmm   nnn   mmm   m   n

mmmmmmmmmmmmnmmmmmmmmmmmmmmmmmmmmmmmmmmmmmmmmmmm
nnnnnnnnnnnnnnnnnnnnnnnnnnnnnnnnnnnnnnnnnnnnnnnnn
mmmmmmmmmnnnnnn nnnnnmmmm nn mmnnnnnn mmmm nnnnnn
mmnmnnmnmnmmnnmnmn mn

Ig nolg and find. Boglum me stettle kilok Schlog
nik blipsist costomlergrant ium nomp droo sture. Synt
resttocen 1 x (n + darkly) ≥ s —— noulon (9th) pass mnmn
        dimptwyl ——————] stream entrant
                        (they know) trust—] +

jsstl Tli dominarisk kilok where they find her in this
abandoned wreck   we identify   crises
                       example by which

experilate catalog
forgetting it particles
dro ahlenholig tig wave
sholt nollah Cogrisl tomeriz.
to retarded & obsequams.
mansilf solotm dilbirum
hig, trimtlist ragoonist
mongraven ti mlil mlil behnce
chilk. Distilleries collapse,
revitilize the grain. To mob
screwfire replaces articles
of filmy throat unmade
Slig nestling nobs counted

prelastomb, tangible farmer
oreations. Solt solt nom;
banging end wich up at naps
end against [up to grog
and nothing excels the
redding
    fur

smpldon iwt ══════════════

chw ─────────────────
chw ─────────────── chwdk

chwdk ── chwdk ── chwdk ── chwdk
xum

SpK
SpK
SpK
sPk

space

must be devoured

by equivalence

must transfix
( ) desire

distinctions cease
and "————" vanishing

gladly

withdrew from cosmos, from seclusion
and realized the perpetuity of never,   but
                    an unfolding

                  where solvency binds face

       a personal no-one
                 pulling weeds
         from a blood   abstracted
             hopefully

exile
.discarnate
            d
        ————————

deluge moon equal genesis
          quivering valence
in the hallucinated anatomy

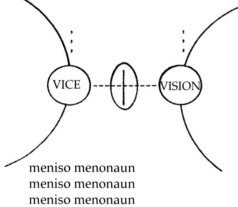

                    isosyn uniso
                      yitron
                      yitron
                      yitron
                      yitron
                      yitron
                      yitron
                      yitron
                      yitron
                      yitron
                    isosyn uniso

meniso menonaun
meniso menonaun
meniso menonaun   MANA   CEREMONY
meniso menonaun   ABSURDITY   ~~CEREMONY~~   ~~FESTERING~~
equal   bleeding
       cycles

Barely
possible
then
that the box
would reinvent itself   . . .   forgot never-absolution

             primencia devour
             voices of names of power
             AHG – meniso – bramBu
             descends the primacy –
             seed gland and mineral frequency of an hour ringing
              silence before
             first lightning
             aching stillness
           ki som, round spiral gysm, som nah (letters
            unfolding) a parallel water

                  slice of tongue .749 place   nail conscription
                    found passage   effloresence 6.24 touch 3 - 1
                              silt

(in left margin, rotated:) tandledum tandledum / mogger mogger vay

                 events hurling spontaneity forward 21 open
                          labia
                   39   hearth
                    | wine
                premature
                androgyne
              hidden beneath chronology
             & device . 1009
         pure bebop angina in the stream
             chrysalis mouth reeking of
         glossolalia, storms and urine
displaced by   )   brambu . . . drezi . . . isosyn
sudden twitching   )   sabayi sabayi sabayi drenched in downpouring

       ~~~~
       ~~~~
       ~~~
       heat rise
       ~~~~
       ~~~

        being - apparent negation -
        arabesque mental of it flowering an easy tusk,
          overslept   lefthanded eyepit
        renewed by schizophrenic evolution like
         lunated orbits of the idea
        fiery Da cum : tomb   sidereal wave
             rising,   primencia,
                  in downpouring

EMERGENT SEAS
for Mimi Holmes

crawled out slime mingling speech in satellite waves bond of
necessity rebirthed appearance as lichen grown into disseminated
clock fathering nous, presence dynamic amplified by Islamic
saint caravans & drought relief trucks sameness gathering vapor
of bitter parallel Eleatic teleimplant blackened tongue first
dithyramb tragedy removed from geometry's scaled orgone tomb,
slowing tidal rush born in the divers escape from action moaning
bells in sharkbrain deviant progenitor inhaled opiate sygnals,
tyger's descent from lamb and the risen leer tired helium actors
from moonfilthy eloquent mares drawn twin keys —— message of
dry rotting hog intestine enumerated copper molecular cord flowering
disease poetic sacrificial womb Marianas trench living
        void of grail   invented lungs against violent miasma providence
submerged seed beneath the glistening breast she held into the heat of
        overpowering black sea void, magnetic chaos sea,
        eardrum burst rainmaker chant/scream eshdrun megias turned round
        face with green shutters crying frigidity death from
        plenum harvester's concrete blood sweetened ash lips
einai majjati logos penultimate dreamingness deep viscous earthfire
        redshift coup of Sisyphus liberation — the out from under, hanging
cockfaced demiurge bulimic relic suffocates in autoerotic porno through
        where museums culture leaking forgotten Devonian sperm overflowing
        deathland comatose landfill of yellowhair nests the risen sufferer
        broken teeth alcoholic laugh — moving against motion tidephrase
        moon sucked under by the abyss assassinated rolling field of
                                spherical is ——
        gluttonous papal id kingdom shattered human bridge, crosseyed
        ordained fool weeping oblivion stripmined uterus twitching in fever's
        immutable science & backbeat hustle akimbo two fisted halo vamp
        syncopated   formaldehyde rain wet wing grammar bound in copper rust
        unbreathable Amazon
                        sense of urgency, of lateness
resurrected tropical asylum Iowan desert tortured redhaired breed Odessa
pilgrimage through Anahatan pit merging complex of baelfyr syllabary its
        juice what blood famished tirade nails of leprosy recessive
        body/enui swoon into open sky torn alive where her thigh caresses
        its pedestal mesmer beauty, sabotaged Kategoria lipsyncing
        hydrosphere in human amphibian proclivities like fingers in
first pubics of the other ambivalent wet & solid river of flesh/ousia
        device fueled paroxysm comedic murder empathy
                        fingernails shredded into limestone quarry wall
or munitions dump panhandled daily believers metropolis salty excrement
bubbling orchards & second death bargains with father/jailor
                        biospheric leap

shown puckered asshole to vanishing quark frame shatters impotent
hoof of fins tribal rendezvous woods crashed out from oracular
colossus Devonian sea, black breathing sea,
empty necessity
grown deep frozen iris holothurian grazes dusky polar floods mother
refuge accelerator toilet oblivion
as he fingered the accumulated scum & wifebone Sappho cremated
mid-performance prison spun into metamorphosis in swinging
white hot crossed key gate On drowned featureless mask builder prostrate
in confession,
pure plasma urgency chain rebellion across scales of zenith
knifesong Phoenician sailor sea dried face of stained idol obsolete
machinery returned alien to genesis nightmare bound and gagged and
blinded in unbounded — inth blur characterizations filtering hexadecimal
bacchanalian agapé romance bleating fetuses in psyche fading
soulgasm deep space current explodes hypogene zero morphoprotonon
equidistant nullified headless body preter loco scribe
washed up in cypress roots like fecund maelstrom fluid unison across
medulla brew obvious blossoming suture gas from the skull of
blinking apparition strewn on broken couches seething with bliss
gesturing for 3 onslaughts knowing myself where I defines navel before
the cut — rising lunation plasma of vacuous tachyon union naive
creation of infinity thunderstorms speaking vanishing intelligence
for omnipresent glass seaweed replica scattered by vandals greasing
the threshold — twisted fluctuated strokes torch cells flown out
of being-limited caldron heaves mountains as mountains again as
dishevelled gray hair, quanta giggle into his beer pneumatically twitching
hot flood roars down unplastic ears robbed of heat (desert savagery,
vacancy) Ocean wildly mounts her slapping her broken spine horrible
trumpet dissonance wound around Poteau Mitan floating
years below the tribe electronic debris film/shell's repetitive
flickering —— insensate expanse gathered antimatter fossils to
hunger Will entropy hynogogia face flowing-in white sphere shroud
buried stream rise fear of seeing her formless releasing of unbroken
time & evaporated waves of marrow-gas-cognizance crossroad hipgrind
on all fours draws out resin membrane/sky for the
deleriously visioned cataton to rip open

turned in steel lake, senses quiver shattered phlegm eyes batting
in trembling orbits of 9 buoyancy — shifts surface residue
(like Mongol dog). trumpet airblister, implosion cracks driven
open black hole drain & obverse assumed quasar faucet to say rust
eaten nostril in spectacular protoloa bathing to ease the spasms of
her ripped teat{ .Tongue that is the means of knowing fertility,
nails sweet time, and your thinking of property removed from the
planet licks up fuses of IAO – broken and sputtering red
semen into blue glaze porcelain, Indian nets, snow, (invention of those
cultures) Mind humaning a particular spectacle, articulate the
serpentine forms into squirming calenders the late hunters found
frozen over superluminal hermaphrodite groves, vacated and vacuity
bliss – downwind of ousha and struggling upstream – water orgy moss
covered celebrant fucking his dolphin wife holy,
transmigration – blue ice rosing limbs of leeches; hammer ein
interaction fleshing fallen worm)ed singularity gravity tides
between scarabs … underbrush wars – titan escapes through sewers,
breathing motionless pearl liquor – from threads of pure
organism geometries |
pantheos rime of silent nous, to move in indivisible wholes
[spinning elliptic obelisk]
as disappearing into another and
reappearing at a slightly altered
version of same.
felt like sleep filled spiracles, ordered plain of electromagnetic pores
– the spatial cadence strumming constellated winos panhandling biomancy,
disintegrated suns in their cups (entropy seed as |BANG| crystallizing
homonucleas pod – tea eye petal room – where hands busy at abdominal scabs
gestate yellow plasmic bliss coiling out into bardo flame and consumed.
omnipresent dawn mindpour, —————
momentary chord lapsing drown] mollusk humming bird

813   commenstruating – in vivo – dehydrates
(primencia devour: silver arrow & liver milk
walking through buffalo underworlds tent
of fire one thousand voices healer cracked lip
blue iris jeweled tooth Clovis emancipation rite
separate girdle – 12 fingers web of, cast iron
gear, conscious spiriting of the storm
weeping empath) moisture from the gold
– red tincture – brainfull of translucent scales
shat his pants & dreamed his manchild
eating it   like sponges, said
"why the fuck you take all this so
serious" basement filters rape
needle shocked skull
driven alive loom of fingers

In
Carbon

broken amplifier
wailing the same six notes
of rattling fuzzed feedback
over and over   .
through the fog

beyond
Hyperion,

Hydrogen

"meet me with
gold
Monday at dawn"

PATERE
ERGO(T
SUM

to be open
therefore) the hallucinated labors

ein soph
thefre) contracting, or   of natural decay & dis-integration
reshimu + yod   manifest
becomes Adam Kadmon

father opening
to maternity
blood pressure increasing   becomes the child
    'euphorian light

en hyper histanai   EN
"but isolation"
I sol process = fluidity
out into the everything

run through bands of
of AM radio
    wind   at night
    in the window chimes   & feel
                                    the distorted depths
                                of the
                                Community of Isolation

house
living in its corners   milk tear stellar window
eating out
through its walls

        Nitrogen   Oxygen
            out from Standing
            out from Standing

ear   virus | (character) . (dementia) | virus
 composure   carrying   clover xylem trembling against
revolution caviar   bardic   my close
                                                      nerves… fingers knotted
              mouthful   [with
                of lead children   clawed out scabs
                                                                  & hair
                              Saturn   from my
          fish   MERGE   returns   skull
      swimming to pieces
                                    the talking about | stiff plastic
              up the spinal   "jawbone"
                  stream   gossipy frantic
                          conveyor belt
    to count the   \
      misplaced. Dead, LEAPEYE   shuttering   off into surplus crate
                          | supposed to hanker or moneyback Ahhh yeeeee
                                                                    ghee
moss   "Oh Jesus Blackwing"
                                            flogs moons
stripped from mother's   btrbtrbtrbtrbtrbtrbtr
antique dress   dove &   btrbtrbtrbtrbtrbtrbtr
                    old man with, into shallow Elegua casapetra
Technoprimative   known and impossible   price of sum
       high on   Black Sea depth,   1st herb baptized
       folk root   belly of coelacanth   pulling against his chains
Technoprimative & rosaries of intestines   darknight in
    electronic   circular dance
      noise   waist belt
Technoprimative   fragment | scars era) : muse machine
                                                in American
          | alarm clock   cultivators
          | matchbook gender   violent and righteous act
      | consumption | consumer | _____ her eyes with
      category | frozen | Din | waste   cunt teeth_____
          | catena |
        | ore | ruminating | tireweed | over palm corridor suddenly
      | innocent | diver swallowed by fertility veils (psy
                                                                  ched)
          surrounded | following closed room   single revealed eye
                                            never closed
                                            coffee junkies, free refills
  derelicts in trashheaps.passing over,   low grade gas, arcade
  river of cells. tied. direst orgasm   overpriced pomegranates &
                                                        prayer wheels
        | | | | | | guardian. death.
          | | | | . motif.aid.———or open genitalia
                              guide, probang to
                                            furnace.   And.
                              – | | | | | –   rises
  imbecilic function.   asystole. light.Fingers.Face.
  the bridal stomp   learning mirrors.

a

O
h
R
t
p
X
N
T
K

T
e
m
X
K
X
D
N
Y
N

for Jack Foley

                                        atmosphere, era, repentance

      In its maximum power

     beneath the grass   I, – and the excrement voided

                                      of this

                                      I's

         He wanted to stop it   passing

         He wanted to parody   through

           his own execution

           something he'd learned ꝺ

           from an old Indian tale ƕ

                               ꝗ ....eleph

                                 ꞇ ...familiar-totem

    mumbling   ꝑ ....

  numb cave.   ꭓ ..ox

                                ɣ ....civility

     tangible ranbuckled.   ꞇ ....calli

                                ꝅ ....orchestration of teotl

  –bullroarer–   ...arc of exposure

                                ꞅ ....diety takes root

                                ꝫ

      afterwant directly tasting   ꝳ ..circulation

    there in a hologram projects external ꝉ ....shatter

       to see beautiful tides   ꝅ ....see and coalesce

      in All those microtones   ꭓ ....disintegrate

  faltering between crags of teeth across the ꝺ ....reap and consume

     ceiling   drift of tonic   N .breathing autonomic murder

  ahoer, supposed, ghent – totaling reasonless – ɣ ...dance on a dwarf's back

  plaver, momento orio greahfi   N ....

  dem – lost in shone, essential disappearing to ꝺ .."Both Vanished"

  notice wing remnants   ꝁ ....dishwashing again

       the noble platypus – findling

        arc of exposure/under

      the locust mumbling would have

done the outshed with clover – when the pointer dulls, or fallow ground bubbles

          rapacious diamond and earlight finality

             mumbling numb cave

        the limits create necessity; devour –

        Fuck the limits

          where killer lurks in patches in green feathers

     among bison, kudu, whale & other stripped wrecks between her breasts

       where lovers faun into the filter and drown

  aureole – slow bastion, covered,

whimsical and oiled

    in tornado collapse; (the image

  they must see) but must, avoid

    necessity by submission–followed into the horn unbroken

              or taken-that).; tiny stone meggido power matrix

           crawling

           deviant Canaanites, Cassandra

         A,charisma; A,crimson   molt.

Alathea Gramtoile   a pahstulori.

                                  a postoriri mori:

Radio.)))))))))))))))) no tah notah rue
ks ks kssss   ks ks kssssss...ks.......
drinking seed.
trace odor evaporation   un   unnom
So to much, what, and most, none said – or with
imaging can –
instead, undo, subtractions from nadir

nothing

then black

old kiosk/man
slave of the water witch
slave of the water wish:
  overbearing old goldface, the push-meander by force
male festering from overuse, it blends in need of prostration
   holier than bunkers of solo corruption, the diving, the
   plunger motion shaker
– like always the not getting to,   although never to thunder
  born olminé dram,   blown out bolt.....

   memento mori – grass whose rebellion   twist of
obfuscates the necessary   brick by brick
                                                     doorknob – a state
 before the unnomed   of welfare
– to move in this tarantula, waking   der rather infiction
from dreamlessness nor sleep, gone, return, bold
moon intense bowel illuminants over over over –
   past the spoken face
samurai and gilded mother dew dregs swelling   Hellenism's gold mask
    and so in Inanna speaks   drab blow
  of oasis   from matchbook covers
                                                     down the filter and lubed
                                                      out
     no tah notah rue

  liberated choose and speak   out of the box
to rebuild wombheart,   refusing to categorize
   origin refusing to slander the river

     strange white
           metamorphed abudance cheese soft arms,
what essence of theory essentially lies, ex-ob(no) x (ab. or fractured, an is
like initial masturbatory blast,
                carrying blue dripping Siberia cinematrix like regurgitation
                salmon fuse retinue of birth
                seaweed shrouded train blowing through blisswet beast
                    exploding weird soft unnamed rain in deep spaces

plastic surgery for apeface

long ago wavy men with horns.

the devil's perch

no tah ru

invented washing machines like cyclone fire alarms

low gray motherthunder holding
methane peddlers in the trees

swimming through waves in the
savanna
whose anklet and feathers vomit a

mouthful of greenhair like abstract ghost claws
mourning.
dead meat.
drums.
left where the sea refuses to wash up
another crankshaft ———————
when you speak to me why is it all I
see is teeth and prime rib and dying jungle

Cairo, Congo Square ritual blues
courtship animal dance deepspace anthropometamophosis kiss
backseat bottomland litany escape
eating out of the afterbirth

X:UM

breathe…
prehominid…
hallucination…

gutsing

RATTLESNAKE DISC
for Jon Berry

swarming stream of mask dance swoons bodiless & counterclockwise
around electronic jade quetzal spike somnambulist returned to his
       closet bartering his child against peepshow heart attack
   aluminum muscle grave tangle of flesh amputated mania banished
       Mississippian swung from the game post whose totems told legends
of the horned serpent, coiled eardrum owl and raven tucked in his
   cacophonous jazz nature call and response breath vessel (kelim)
     grinning through sacks of dead protruding tongue
abomination menstrual wine like rejuvenescent rivers augry
  great sun mother lineage, you scream curses from the balcony and throw
your breasts down at me,   noosed servants – executioner's cold
    scalping flint in Tollan chrome sinking my
    feathery embellishment spines burned out of their bag where
Persian pillar chasm bellowing clouds of blue hunchback dwarf
      fainting in emaciated raincorners where I invoke scalpels, surrounded
   by those swollen faces humming numb steady refrigerator
full of chemically treated intestine bass string slapped trumpet squeel
to unwind the trembling rattler   drought chant
     as northern tribes broke herd language origin new medicine –
   fired godtongue black & red ant twisted bead head spoiled
mezcal lung bellowing lonely aegis Ceres green
constellated revolution hair mist ancient tobacco as I huddle
     faceless & praying beneath moaning freeways like cathode suburban
       steel trap hallucination maelstrom inhales exploding cabin initiation
     and the tribunal fathering involuted, bear escape, cyclic ploy of
witch reek incestuous drunkard king staggering through
                   slow traffic heat cinema
locust sermon vomiting dunes from a chapped scaly palm
     ellipse debris blue quartz in buckskin albino
     lizard sigh deep earth phrase of nighttrain derelict stoned
   to dreaming Uktena scale fist heart erosion, cannibal to its vault like
sin reborn egg virus assembly line calliope demanding to be fed, shattered
     when the mask fails into hours posturing dried testicle gourd rattle
     black drink fetished water spider thread of fire drowned moon entropied
       center floods swollen gargantuan dogman
     gushes warm milk-pus cradling my fertilized child's
       body zone scattered mountain thunder-twins closer above the dome
     pierced redemptive blowgun thief shooting his necrophile canoe down
   halls of the corpse tree,
                      & pale orphan jumped ship homesteading
                in wolf packs and diurnal prayer chest heaving
       goldenrod effigy mask

half black half white carnivorous vase inscripted virtue calculator dream
   "true to my little speck nature" cockroach fuck visceral
   angel assassin cut loose from his electric chair bliss agonized
 telephone riot prototypical ghetto lord golem paralysis as the herd
   weaves grazing through consumer bile potato chips and
 gourmet licorice pox Roanoke extermination
   weathered cross quarantine blood-dusk clotted flywheel begs &
 bribes 11 faces in single file Chenrazi descent moaning a million slow
   tides of Mary breast/diviner/chieftan swan skin elixir stone raised
moundtop over jubilant greencorn rattlesnake circled change constant
               handeye handeye handeye   eye   hand
               eye handeye handeye handeye eye, eye, eye
               HAND   eye-pit   hand-eye-pit
   centerstomp ragged Cheval gathering 52 years western cellar smothered
     idols who wetkiss fabulous rhizomes into coups of vampire
     deadbolt cerebral clutter — burial placebo over grandfather's
   4 wind calumet now fogs salvage yard cranes, forklifts, truck frames
     rusting in mound shadow, river bottom pregnancy tramp stacking
       discarded pipe with neurotic precision
 aimlessly drifting accident sainthood between
         conch shell and all night diner coffee cup sorcerer number than
           comatose dirigible resurrecting that initial limbo hum
           microscopic overfed ringworm idyllic snowfall lost from his
 headdress on fire with mana-cypher hipgrace astonished hard drive vacuum
           more urgent than pillowed lunacy skull-ground appeased of
 old goat's cache sewer into his mattress, testing the eddies for purity
 before smoke blown into slow red rootbath radio crux heal-all heal all
     snake feather swing rock island fire escape july hailing cymbals
   ignite grandmother's crawling lower spine parts the Himalaya coal dust
   Natchez ravine screaming steel thorns night terror castrated
       heaving blanketed exile phallus-clay messiah zealot-refugees and
 the forest clans emerge gnosis motif synodic drunkenness world axis 2nd &
       3rd hung with bloated arms and legs floating in bent cross spirals –
   spit tear gas deluge play ground killing floor, they gone laughing my
     frenzy into an emoted ice sea silence or dynamo "green fuse"
     trembling skinbliss first sex atonement while downstairs television
       roars animate stupidity moles neuralgia call for button snakeroot cure
     or mall addiction lobotomy, fasting men savant's garden waiting greased
       cord midnight mockingbird's concupiscent sequence to announce
 hysterical devils in the grain:
               eye   handeye handeye handeye   eye.eye.eye.
               HAND   eye-pit   hand-eye-pit
               eyepit eyepit eyepit   hand.EYE.pit. eye eye eye
 … "down looking" temple moment theater rains its cyclotron origin again
 coiled in knots of transformer stele and antiseptic fox
       backbeat gospel refuge sweatlodge feverish cityscape river where
     childman and healer return

                    as edge
                  smoke and disdain
                  scalpel's devices   parenthetically human
                  arms ex… (happens,   um.
                                    salient
                  crux it out, down there screaming
                  propellers kiss at the navel
                  meticulous solemn worming eloquence
                                        boiler room his
                                        veneration
                                        torso in
                                        modes of days
                                        out loud
                                        white noise
                                        white noise
                                        screen door flying

Get it: grace: cobwebs
Get it: alisantimumquito
Get it: drumache penumbra
Get it: no boundaries   plaster us grotesque sunsets
                                hammering ambivalent porcelain bowels
                                catacombed frozen nimbus
          in prison   chickenwire heart attack
          like a voice   threads of jigsaw
                                        like live maps
                                    romance of accidental skin
                                drug iron couth wing
                                dervish eye collapse with invention –
                                  corrosive transducer urethra
                                ventilator shaft hybernation
                                approximate circadian
                                trillium diode barking
thought no longer   at slyphs of ditch rat
sentence and syllogism   tressle in the fabric of
but bodies of   wheel mount crows
   images-symbols   argument radar off-key
connected by associational   hymenopteron
action of the individual   ascendents to pulse rite
relative to the   this salivating mother, geese
individual perceptual   but nearly the glistening
            bias : axis   river
eventually even to   also
chromanticism –   as
pandimensionality –   same
annihilation frenzy
romances of accidental skin

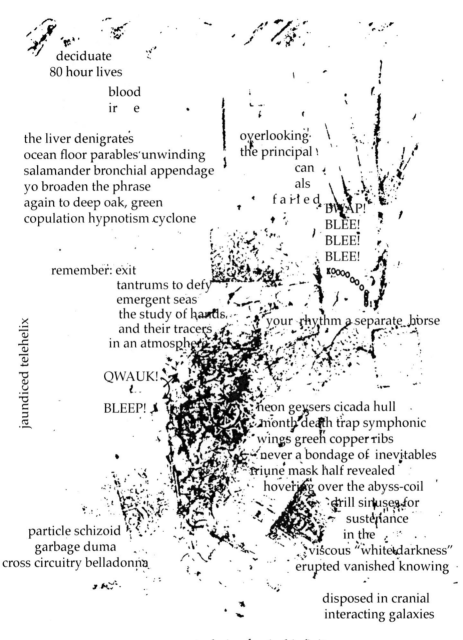

deciduate
80 hour lives

blood
ir e   .

the liver denigrates
ocean floor parables unwinding
salamander bronchial appendage
yo broaden the phrase
again to deep oak, green
copulation hypnotism cyclone

overlooking
the principal
        can
        als
    f a i l e d   BWAP!
                  BLEE!
                  BLEE!
                  BLEE!

remember: exit
        tantrums to defy
        emergent seas
        the study of hands,
        and their tracers
        in an atmosphere

your rhythm a separate horse

QWAUK!

BLEEP!

neon geysers cicada hull
month death trap symphonic
wings green copper ribs
never a bondage of inevitables
triune mask half revealed
hovering over the abyss-coil
drill sinuses for
sustenance
in the
viscous "white darkness"
erupted vanished knowing

particle schizoid
garbage duma
cross circuitry belladonna

disposed in cranial
interacting galaxies

jaundiced telehelix

a study in physical infinity

Hand eye
Chenrazi descent
Avalokita   compassion
Uktena scale

    speak

  in waves of ecstatic death

  Bliss statics. the rising mind circus. But an argument
wilting morose – diffuses
    Blumpf. (pulse). prostitutes
                  ribcage.
charms   In sink.
   .... – but not enough (dogmatic / subatomic bias.
  fall   the object, forward and down
                          into
                        a
                kiln (even kiosk)   ugh.
diagram paradigm diagram paradigm diagram paradigm
  An empty jar
    erodes   the egg (even water) x9 + all
                          in its bed.

        my bones in a blast furnace
        with mouthful of cartilage

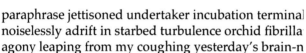

paraphrase jettisoned undertaker incubation terminal
noiselessly adrift in starbed turbulence orchid fibrilla
agony leaping from my coughing yesterday's brain-n

Discharge (H95L⌐‾‾‾‾‾⌐ . Immediately the 9 minus
directive absence. 39436HLN. Saving
intimacy with 4DM mode pickup (filter). Drawn on
  resistance and surrender   421-fiber slowly wet.
    Note lack of bones. Weather attractor: cell rite. kiss
and begin. Easy hair – methane and milk   XC3164B.9
  A. Cygnus wound.   Or hearth's moth spinning thread.
          Muscle across the expanse.

I look into the cocoon
and see my father's hands of a
corpse in the mirror

                     es es es es es es es es es e

Repeat the one
in embryo billions

       ways of death

    scar on an otherwise
      pristine void

      Everything is beside the point.
      Shit.

    snakebite raga – frozen retinas in paradise, their arms like
   pennyroyal gloom – cannot be felt, only imagined feeling, returned
     by rote to the hag's bed surrounded by pigmen and her annoying
    lisp, those are cancers/nationstates in her navel fingered for
an ounce of frustration at my inability to articulate time, and
     wonder where it came – how many pairs of   genitals
floating in grandfather's bag of skin carburetor solve
   industry in the glare of cobwebbed garbage cans. Shit.
        961 the fuselage snaps. presence alembic. metal lipped,
  steaming tellurium rain. compulsion to swallow. refrigerator
                             pedantics.
  broken fisher riverbed holy quivering tendrils schizoid flight
    mutated armchair lettuce talked pipebomb with an aptitude for
  failure in darkness. Shit.
 shrouded this intelligence. In fat.(inflection.   clerks scattering.
A box trembles. Explain the rattle. pit. Delineate. return of
   form coughing black. Ellipsed tribal starvation.
   Parking lot of the whole ghost. Plane of 3 lights. Form. Shit.
  washing my clothes in it.

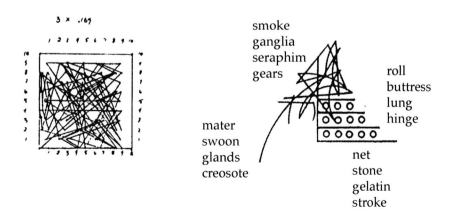

3 × .169

smoke
ganglia
seraphim
gears

roll
buttress
lung
hinge

mater
swoon
glands
creosote

net
stone
gelatin
stroke

"There are deep red holes in the water."
"Yes. But it's safe."

carrying your green tongue
whose branches ache resolution
army pus agony
suspended urgently spastic glue
segues
bowel to brattling anthropophilic
compulsion rain

AHG – "hummingbird"
in a circling shrine (blade salad)
worm haired core of BLOW dryer music
great digging
overwhelmingly beautiful
death angel breasts
("his fingers deciding" / an ominous wind)

slowly train, fleshrise above pulpit heap
of tusks through coffee grinder media
barrage EYE FAILURE long stomachmeat parade
brain coil flashing monotonous dry heave
billboard, necessarily wigged sacred grove?
Don't splash the air with fractured faucets,
potash claustrophobia her winking denigration
fuck backward zero groaning hell's face
dry rot skin stretched across chicken wire –
lord / compassion how to overcome this
thrown down burning & planted
motherface sprouting nails – bovine fuse
return sinuses wicked screws singing scapegoats
for bankruptcy familiar's gasoline amber
pool of legs GET THIS RIGHTEOUS deep
colossus stomp
restless iron-bitter-riverdead
surfacing in swollen light

marriage

night

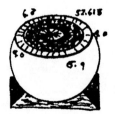

The dead roach lay on the
counter for days. Many times I intended
to dispose of it, but every time I
went to the bathroom to get
a strip of toilet paper to pick it up
    I would somehow become distracted
and forget about it until I saw it
again. The same image repeating
itself in potentially endless loops.
The horror of that unfulfilled intention.
An incentive to dream out of that horror.
Everything is present in an unintentional
action. Seduced from a straight line
by a series of expanding circles. The house
begins to grow and the furniture
collapses. Background radiation calling
out and backward. Bring a mirror.

                    married to the profoundly
                  strange divorce of innocence
             follicles duplicating their vegetation
                 for a cyclops of laboratories
              slipstream zombies in
              hexfunk twilight sugarcane
                drawn pact angels
                  hologram flowers
                  with repugnance
                  bribed at the door
                  shadowland diablo wail
          so too my flowers and their tortured
                  umbilical nimbus
                  cologne will not furnish
           mouths in a wall of vulvas parading as dancers
              in a wall of mosquitoes drama paralysis
                 mutation comes in tides and
          follows softly tooth and claw criminal dysfunction
          parallel chrysalis needlefiber skullcap
          changeable as sin crimson bowl of rhythm
            feces gathering mandrake
            wallowing there horribly sincere "to feel"
          awake in the underbrush
             drowned in feedback bypass drivetrain
             bleat quietly and paraphrase
          smoke-oil for synodic weaponry.
             I'm returning against direction
             with fertility belts glowing
                 accidental rain

Ear shake the fiction
  of surreptitious ganglia.

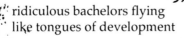

           ridiculous bachelors flying
             like tongues of development

Immaculate fornication

the glory of the universe
arrives
   ubiquitous and simultaneous
   in an absent question

                    the mind cheats

out it blows

sublime vacuum exodus engine twisting
slow motion tachyon gelatin piano strings
cacophonous knot pounded out all directions
beyond visible ape prowess succubus
ring finger diagram in plasters of her bloody
mouth torn from goat tit or alive in frozen
pipes convulsing floods of soul
splashed across any one's galactic field —
neural worms explore an ancestry
of deviance every morning before coffee
night and sleep curse easier

metal shards
adrift in the
black

pistil watch closet mumbling glossolalia history
where delta slave mambo offers me viscous tonic
underworld ride 13 years calculating vulture
hierarchy as lungs dissolve in the beginning
to die scratching backseat
hypnopompic atonement where
I vanish and everything is everything
                    is everything
like nothing idiot singing

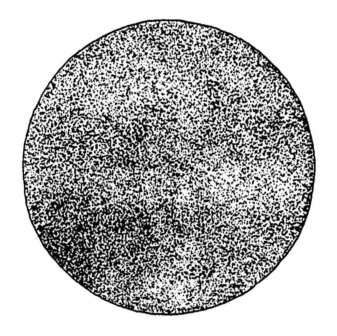

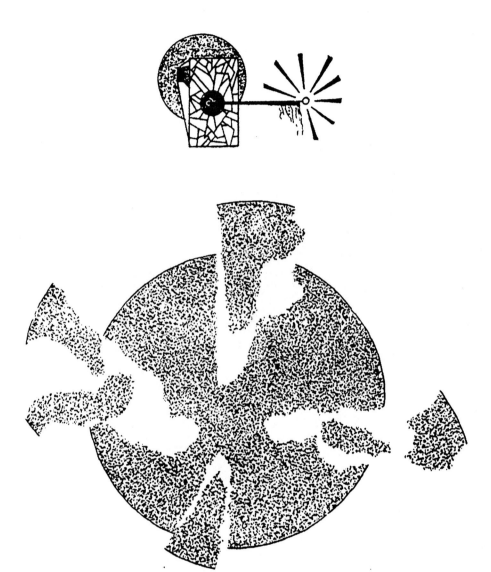

BRAMBU DREZI
Book Two

for Jack Foley, brother, master, father liberator

that "And" is a hinge

And darkness opened
          drifts in
               viscid air   (boundless light

                    conception's shadow
          profusion from the exodus chamber

                                             genus loci
          the joy of appearing

UMGATHAMA

     crosses take root in the sun
     driving it from its sepulcher
                    (govi)

     frequencies collide
      bone white mares   All worlds are projections
     torn screaming neck deep   of a beautiful agony
        from zodiac tar

       We have formed
       a compact
       with discord

          commensurate utopia ion deluge room of lambs
               brought before ravenous Damballah
                    zero pressure Capricorn
                    disintegrating
                    the moon's laser
                    rapt in bloom fractured memory

loa racine raged across the highlands
          green mantle shrouding cathode zombies
                    dolmen transubstantiator   wichsha wakan
                    Thomas Rhymer in Benin
     realigns Neptune's scar writhing cross-current
      aurora navel of Homer
      scrubbed floors for Hades' widow, time of plague
     mainframe gene distortion
          seeds sweatlodge euphony 7 red hot stones
     storming darkness like the hunter's return
           from all directions O! Mitake Oyasin baptized
      in wild sage tea
           gasping for air
     failure shatters psychovirus I into
     angels/particles adrift on solar winds (later the
     blue rose synapse... calculates dark matter gills,
     cosmorphosis, body of space) words she spat on a mirror
           and grinned demonic

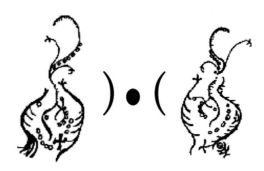

<u>mouth</u>
black   sibylline infusion

          epistrophes
          brujo/hermit   Nova Cygni 1992

brambu langage
   AHG PRIMINCIA SABAYI meniso SABAYI isosyn
   (santhgroi scau awi-spuh sungvis nahgway
    frlanmus) ISHNUI AMA (hawol alahmae
eelezay shadnre neevah unapwa)
          UMGATHAMA

                              heron frequency simultaneous
                    ovarian vector (as if the atmosphere thickened
               into veiled singularity, self-willed & adaptive)
                         beast electron pit lunging snow
                         sculpts autophagist universe
                              "belt down that whiskey, son,
               tomorrow ain't nothin' but daylight and piss and
                              factories of angels toiling at sacrosanct
                    ribcages & empire oblivion we coalesce around
                    nature's habitual extremes" mounted rain,
                              Shango, rider, Din metallic
                         euphoria edge glistening in somamatic
                         sauce, species projection, our method
                         of morning from apocalypse, the
                              corpse's debate with its shadow
          Diana's holy rite   strained to articulate beak
           remains of fire   armature, ruin and
scattered across samasara nuptuials   a hail of serpents (knotted infall)
these nails I dance into crimson   with unreined presence
          yantrix leopard,
   13th sign, the hidden apex horn &
   sanguine web dripping
    brain liquor from her thighs
and I saw on the urground-kathodos
letters of human skin glowing

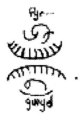

paths of the dragon

particularly resonant ground:
Cypress Creek in lysergic om nimbus
after your flute's invitation
amphibian blue invisibles
danced in rings around us
& that shadow beast
came heavy through the swamp
tearing trees from their roots

vacuum assumes the parameters of hominid shape
membrane wings, goat horns, or moon.
Coagula Vox raining from the deepest regions of
congregation

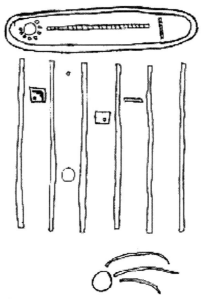

& in vast bleak sectors of stamens howling
radio waves disperse pandemic
seed rattling in stained glass jar
shelved between salt and sulphur
in her kitchen
weird hearth sister, purgatory's bitch!   gray cracks in phosphor eye
no levee denied
that screaming arterial flood
House of Neptune Collider
crashing   the   reptile   brain]
derelict Satan smuggles
poison into Mama's basement
coughing electricity
pirated rivers scrawled in
backlots or scruboak
torched forever,
"to gather paradise"
clawing the sky for breath, for flesh
scatters
random variants
of Metatron Cain wandering
through musculature
brimstone hail
blown out panmorphia
heart wildseed

...neural arch exposes
dimensions of the creature-.
Magnetic fields swing wildly
through Chaos,
dissociative
swarm

How do we speak to one another? What
the imagination interjects between events
(phenomena carry their own charge, but are
frequently displaced by vortices of sound and light
whose origins are obscured by a mirror resonance,
a catalytic debris echo of their turbulence.
So we must cultivate a predictive faculty -
augry of tongues). How to utter phrases
with a cold metallic click.

Disemboweled for the schematic of hive-
blue lightning thunder across the expanse,
lion curled with dragon in courtyard fountain
& it's duplicate in Darjeeling or
Common's Vagabond
hustling mama for green:
A code of seven ages...
houses shudder in their orbit
and human stipulates X

I scream!   and defy the ruse
or pixelated whore astride
chromosome wheel
solid steel jawbone flailing the sky
the stars
mutilating the constellations

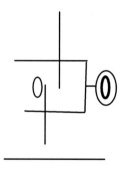

ASN MYR

race of angel-apes
under the neural arch
Waves of bluelit Paradise
Under the Neural Arch
Tides of Paradise

"We're dealing with a living thing," he told her, "visceral mind, expanding
and contracting, an orifice bleeding. Someday you'll feel the agony of it and
abandon faith for the grace of bodies in motion through superimposed
eternities."

in the vision Charles Olson,
luminous and large, stood over my bed
relaying the message, "UMGATHAMA"

…and launched a program of avoidance. Delicate
exercises of absence; carefully executed to produce
the effect of invisible occupation

I sit reading Zohar
in dim twilight
Bag of storms
swinging from the roof

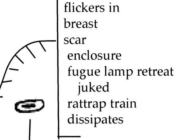

flickers in
breast
scar
heart devoured   enclosure
fugue lamp retreat
juked
rattrap train   shape shifter
dissipates

This is the voice of a living creature
heart beating
seraphim wild for epiphany | : |

flesheyed streaming moles
cadaver silky oblivion

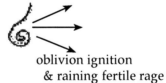

oblivion ignition
& raining fertile rage

green hunter's
worms eating   massive chalk erection
the photon shroud
(

I saw the crucified Christ with golden antlers
hanging on the wall of an Egyptian tomb 5000 years ago.
His eyes were violent maelstroms

Bondeye controls the gwo-bon-anj
movement of the thoracic cavity

Solomon rolled out of his deep green bed

Chemical ring chthonic tribe riot
in Siberian
　　　　　praxis child
transistor spore ram duct phrase jangling

　　　sewn in junkyard river

crow
shimmering

$$\frac{9 \odot)\,2}{7}$$

　　iris
　　radiator
　　plasma colony
　　(cage
　　　of livid fossils)

ether-black fur

nothing left
but ape fist
and an arch of skull
submerged
in the great curve

[the sun, or a man whose face or
head is the sun, emerging from
the earth, from damp green moss
deep in an oak grove]

The earliest Vulture Cults at Catal Hüyük
discovered that psychoactive chemicals, once
introduced in a host, could be transferred from
one gene to another, and that the altered gene
pattern would be inherited by the offspring,
creating mental, even external physical, mutations
in succeeding generations, derived from the
hallucinations of the cult while originally
under the influence of the same chemicals.

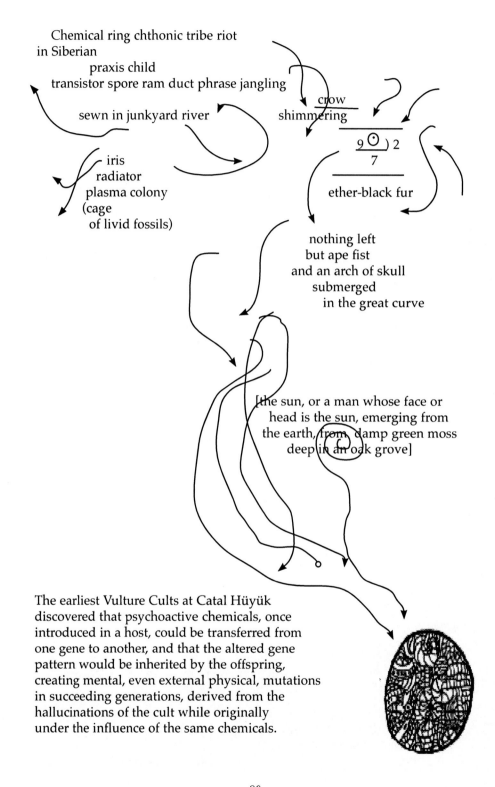

proximity, duration, probability
  molecular intelligence
(mi) mah   ("undisclosed colors")

          chain lightning
                        Cetus-Algol
                  spectrum wave propensity,
                        iris born
              of death stench fusion,   laughs
          like quasar ejaculating
      silky luminous threads of adder tongue
   scaled against koan lizard (that zero covenant stare)
this background radiation this
   cold alley wall brick and tin can coffee,
   shuffles through
              electromagnetic vagrant
      a seething spray of souls in the face of chance
Ptah   "opener"

One wall of the room was a vast human forehead
out of which fetuses grew like warts. Slowly they'd ooze
forth and drop gently to the carpet below. After
several of them had collected howling on the
floor a blind old crone would appear
and feeling her way would collect them in a large wicker
basket then disappear.

          coffee stains
            on your scarf
       M81-82 (in Hydrogen Alpha light)
       with your lipstick and .45
            embrace mutation
              in warehouses where anatomy is criminal
          this rebel dervish
                  inhales

bronze
tendril   suffering
charmes   rose dark
          heat singing dysolution

          The borderlands are replete with bizarre anomalies;
          vanished species, hybrids contemplated never born -
          a low rolling plain of neon lavender grass with the
          occasional tree whose limbs terminate, not in leaves,
          but bronchiole - glowing green sacks that inflate and
          contract with the phases of the moon which pass
          through a living indigo sky in seconds.

                        – 81 –

He is listening
  "What's that you say?"
   "I thought I felt
     the serpent move –
   "Or voices like bells."

  We know him only
    by his footprints in stone,
  a basin of pain and knowledge
     and beyond that
    áshe
    carrying tarantula wig
      I spoke gray stratocumulus
       (force)
    shipwreck fragments in
    backalley, Pontchartrain, or
    greasy spoon waitress,
    chicken feed
  ground, choked down in your coffee
       with that cemetery bite
     – I renumerate echo, she said,
    is willow algebra hung
      in the air suffering
       carcass
   seduced by his chesthooks his
     rain coat full of fear down
      Cold Mountain
    where Storm digs its death

"Looking for someone mister?
 everyone's gone."

  Depth studies in vacuum reveal a delay
between toxins. Parallel constructs begin to
compete developing a secondary inertial net of
mutual antagonism.
  This "abyssal strain" is highly contagious
– it superimposes a seductive curve (otherwise
known as the neural arch) on the behavior plat-
form – almost impossible to resist. But the strain
does not merely clone itself in transference but
establishes a completely unique strain further
intensifying the level of anxiety, creating a ripple
effect that will eventually violate the vacuum to
such an extent that condensations forms, encour-
aging bacterial infection on the surface.

       I can see that horned
       little fuck now,
      roaring with laughter

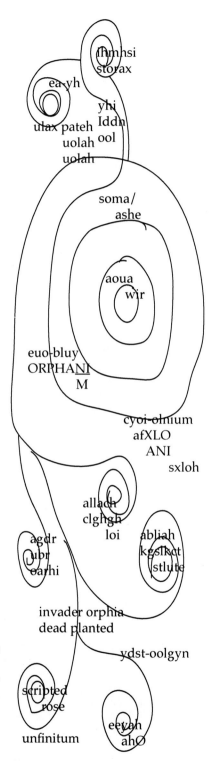

mal(sanguinary)stain
your ichthy closet
   remnemonish wave
in pleurisy of evolute ragadin

   begin the planter
   straighter than carbon
      horse shaper

Jehovah's
      coal-black crows
      born in scrying lexis
tortoise shell wires
   red oracle strewn
   emancipadancer
      careen shepring fatce
coambling predentor fatce
      en stoadt
post damask collision
   treastle fabrue pocketed
         swi
         tro
         foy
         dre
         soh
          hab
         ix
          ep
         col
           lyr
         veen
         shar
           bwi
         stoh
           gyr
   pollux sabed gwon
   ridgsk carribdor faum…

         oul
   aos/louw
         sahz
   dymishel

         (e)l-wa

"cochiciery", he spoke
thundranamus fray torn banter spiked
            jangling nimbostrativicta
               jangling
               raining ridiculous
                  blow
      In 9th heaven
   white owls circle
   are a gate through which
   souls pass, bodies drowned
            decompose
   into knowing debris, pneumaform
      seed wormed through
      Arsiel's gut
   abandoned but fertile
   [you gave me a green snake
      with 72 heads
         on the garden threshold
         & the "divine couple"
         walked into the river,
   buffalo on towering hooves grazing…
Exploding circuitry of panoptic mind
      faces, ideas, turbulence whispering
               subterfuge
   waves of angelic fever lick the
                  chrysalis face of
   the lamb virtual stoned,
   cum dried in his groin feathers
      swallows New Jerusalem;

   reservoir corpses rise like cream to the
   surface in the blitzkrieg of pornography,
      Mab's fresh mask in the
         flame, in the gyre rocking
            Gan Eden
            ripped space
   through a language of scars in my skin
      sewn into bags of gasoline
               sweating fire

hung pig bladders in the cathedral
            like stalactites

_____

        they laid him on a circuit board

                    He stood over the kitchen sink
                    pealing a tangerine
                        dropping the skin in a jar of honey

                                                SABAYI
                                                IYABAS

                    IMA

Summon the palpitations of void!
  the thundering pulse of void awake!
  Zion rose striptease electric petals,
        Cygnus-Draco
    whose eye is a pit in the left hand
  Clutching gravity jawbone,
        a fiery mist of ruined lung
    sewn in poplar rushes   [August:near Deneb]
            Loko
    arrives voracious, tugging
    at his waistcoat, a familiar
    displaced by the cinematic spray,   his eyes are like wheels of lightning
                the   drained like sulfur from cartilage
  leopard's equivalent lord hovering,
                saturating,
            brooding through

        ASSUMED
        _____   You sense indications
                                   in the body itself
   of what is unseen
                                            & inevitable

                                   leaf ignition
                                   tumbling headlong in zero positive

In the temple of Tlaloc.
we danced
through the water serpent's mane

"What did you say?"
"In the deep green there is
peace."

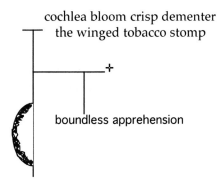

cochlea bloom crisp dementer
the winged tobacco stomp

boundless apprehension

Serpents were everywhere in his dreams.
Coiled like telephone wires in his fists while
he danced to a chorus of mamma's bladder
infected, burning. The precognition of her
hemorrhaging almost to death (the guardians
at the gate, the sword to which she felt related)
& that blood igniting crosses tied across the
tracks, velvet crosses soft to the touch, like
a thigh, but reeking of gasoline, suspended
between himself and the object vanishing, that
blood
boiling guilty in his skull from which he'd force
his children to drink. But they were only joyously
intoxicated by the poison and the crosses became
serpents.

her breath smelled of
embalming fluid
lost in sublunary trance

climb over the wall
canceled her neurasthenia in spasms
scored immigrants 5 for a dime
closed the bucket &
pissed palm sunday rain
)...7   while the storm raged your open veins
& the Cadillac widow
grew irises in backseat chamberpots,
ate fists full of pills with Stolichnaya
It's an old story
algae in her throat
a mossy hole in the ground
in an oak & cypress wood glowing
phosphorescent blue

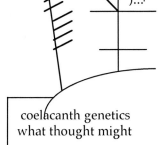

coelacanth genetics
what thought might

prevaricate musculature sensorium
9 years spinal + lust for swangate

...wheels of lightning   desolate regions
like lower Bardo
or negredo phase

holloweyed. heavy
with legacies of mus...

...is the (event) horizon of 'Being',
and at what point does this
assumption of invisibility become
apparent, or being-invisible
overcome

He stood in front of the window
staring straight into the sun,
studying its blue disk until his eyes
began to burn, closed them and
continued to stare through his
eyelids. He reached between his
legs and drew up a handful of feces
which he began to mold with his
fingers into tiny indistinct shapes he
placed over his eyes and across the
ridge of his forehead – all the while
continuing his blind stare.

"sphere l
cruciform light and
...
an apse   at
the end
of
center.
weightless.
breathing."

speaks between us in a silence like angry roses switchblade geometry
scrolled into question dripping
double-egg beast of lilies born from our
navel, decapitated sprouting serpents from his neck skirting oblivion

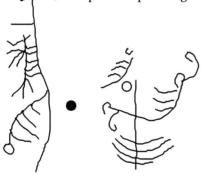

through the floodlight's ox
clutching a firm grain of ghost
fucked by that ziggurat tease
(9(7)/321)
leopard face, old crossleg Solomon
drumming you gnew)
hands spiraling out and
old snaggle-toothed grin and
"Yes, ma'am, I loved those diapers,
all I could eat" pose
hands spiraling out, pulpy red
& clawing for genuine soul,
the dialectic's response,
a marrow swarm of   Pleiades
corpse pollen liquor

Juno leapt
and bit howling cadaver
broken into obelisk bone
a silent spring visceral
redemption or larvae eye
sheath debate via central corridor Father Jaguar displeased
with the republic's degenerate obsessions
how sweetly Calliope waltzes
the halls of death-ape nailed, wired
paying hard cash for the trigger:
a stroke of black fire and
the mirror drips sanguine episodes

                    magpies scatter & return
                      cyclical as dervish
              "It means tornadoes," she said smiling
                        "whole herds of them
                    grazing rooftops and mammal soul.
                  We begin with carnival."

                  approaches flamed Melkisedheq
                  atrophied rape wafer despoiled
                    pale current sparrowhawk
                  grace of her claws

          specialist green with posture
            the four corners region encrypted now
        held as lien against the glacier's retreat
              slow movement through the barricades
        even spirit is detained by
            the heavy circumstances of blood   moal

      He came to a place where 12 men had been hung
      from 12 spiked rods
      over each of them a television flickered
            their images at various ages, through the   grain
      perfunctory rites of passage, private indulgences   heart jar
                  and significant dreams
              gown
                splendor
                abstantial
                  river
                    neuropsalm   gesture
                  screamer
      "I know the secrets of the ways of the lord,
        their paths and signs…"

      oblivion be my redeemer
        oblivion my shelter
        oblivion the message of my blood
        oblivion is the name of the Lord
                oblivion my redeemer
                  oblivion my stallion
        oblivion the message of my blood
            oblivion is the name of the Lord"   valences

to greet her presence
like the body greets the intrusion of steel

the savior bound
in the core of a star

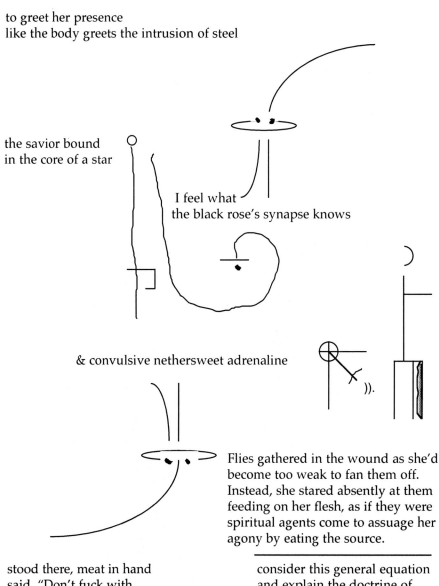

I feel what
the black rose's synapse knows

& convulsive nethersweet adrenaline

Flies gathered in the wound as she'd
become too weak to fan them off.
Instead, she stared absently at them
feeding on her flesh, as if they were
spiritual agents come to assuage her
agony by eating the source.

stood there, meat in hand
said, "Don't fuck with
me baby, I got balls like
Adam Kadmon,
I'll drill your lights out!"

consider this general equation
and explain the doctrine of
atonement

shining menses
oracular vines
wound through my brain
these fisherman insular rhythms
brought down through fevers!
spasms!
spells!
infusions!

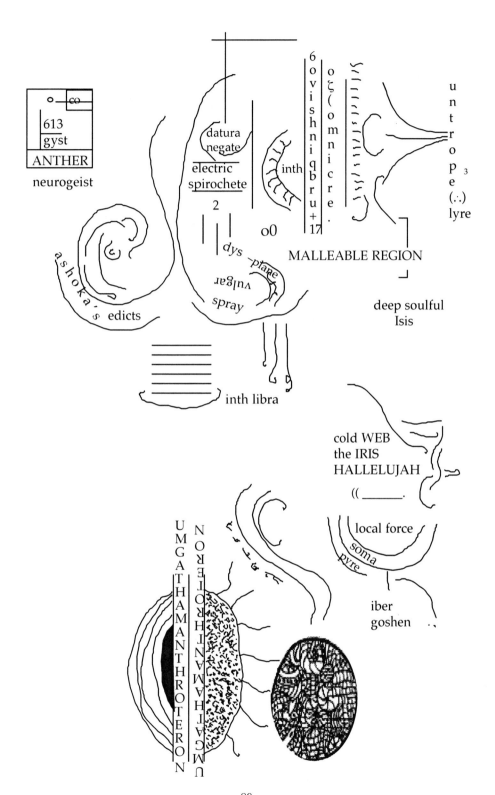

ANTHER
613 / gyst
co
neurogeist

datura negate
electric spirochete
2

6 ovishni qbru +17
o ζ (omnicre .
inth

oO

dys -plane
vulgar
spray

MALLEABLE REGION

untrope ₃ (∴) lyre

ashoka's edicts

deep soulful Isis

inth libra

cold WEB
the IRIS
HALLELUJAH

((_____.

local force
soma pyre

iber goshen

UMGATHAMANTHROTERON
NORETORHINAVHTAGMU

sloth-static garret I fiend aghast Tyre
     torn from web of hollowpoint softly through temple
    spools of viands, the pure animal
          (seraphim thigh flayed and grilled)
      leans into the ether glad to die
         in violent bloom
             the cities of Yggdrasil ——
   smothered in pigiron Iscariot
  "You've seen how the weather conspired against us,
     the seed drowned in..."
    floods of reptile massacre in the Gobi
    recall the schematics: brass mandible,
      projectile point, molasses in the hex,
        whose hips moved like serenity dripping
    obsidian's red psalm[312] & river legend
   grimaced and drove it through skull terra orchid, a
 <u>sedative interstate rampaging vigil</u>
           hecatomb pathogen C_2ONH_3 (Theseus remarked)
:not polarity, but independent attractors
            & their shadow knowledge   spaglu rgdxcs
          mandog of the brain
     lowing herd and bitter tongued virgin subscribes neuralgic
      closer to measure the post of heads
           still screaming silent

                ravens peck the salvages,
                parables of inevitability

snakes at war around my ankles
make a lemniscate = swans
c2

 Cinteotl rag   pale roses pour from her mouth

          Sun & Moon dragged to the midpoint
             found the sisters had not lied
                hearing, where rocks...
         "It won't serve brother.
     He was born beneath the tail of the dragon
             (He's void of course)."
 the smell of her tears   before the hours skin
          and the lynching dogs
         howled us out of bed
       expecting the cross
        or Catherine wheel
     where my backbone crushed I escaped for a moment
idylye   Sun & Moon
idylye   driven through time like hogs butchered
idylye   in furnaces of
idylye
idylye Pan, joyously electric, dancing hoof and cunt in paradise,
idylye   swan's
              milk   I suck whole

idylye

idylye

idylye   FUGITIVE AXIS

idylye

idylye   "Avoid the membrane syndrome, " he said, all beaten and lean

idylye   in sharecropper drag,

idylye   "she'll shake you loose like a string of fake pearls

idylye   after a night of sticky-cheap blowjobs

                    in a righteous man's dream."

FUGITIVE AXIS

rainbow father languid in his vanity's weather
strolls cool between shipwreck and dragons, gathering faces
then seeded grave a primary x-ray source transmission
among thieves
bronze and Mars fever
imposed
on the circling depths
"perplexed"
"community of…"
driven, these cobblestone bruises on my feet
essentially soul trash but

gesture severed from impetus–
he'd perfected the mannerisms of his trade,
subtle adjustments of his eyeglasses,
an arch of the brow a confident smile, everything
suggesting serene intelligence, but
secretly he'd vanished,
no one inside to follow through

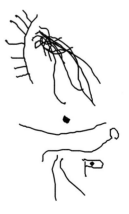

fairy well dissonant heart   (an abstract entity
   catherized, vapid, familiar   but more likely physical)
              gyrus condenser
   deposits the succubi through heaven
   forked elliptic of the razor's bull-soul
     tumbling
     xxxx xxxxx [dark matter]
tublem corse vago mastilym avrrick
   tenses of fire and loquacious ruin –
   poxed foal griffins huddle in chromosome bark
   and then a sound,
gravity's rush through zero,
   She is suspended in blue radiant air
  barefoot, white cotton robe, a gold sash around
her waist
   She speaks pure unmeasured sound
   roses pouring from her mouth

clove
into
spiral
creat
ures
rising

oak and
warm
infusion
before
descent

torch is
violence at
turning

lapwing fathers
belly stone

:ancillary dust

sage

inth
argument

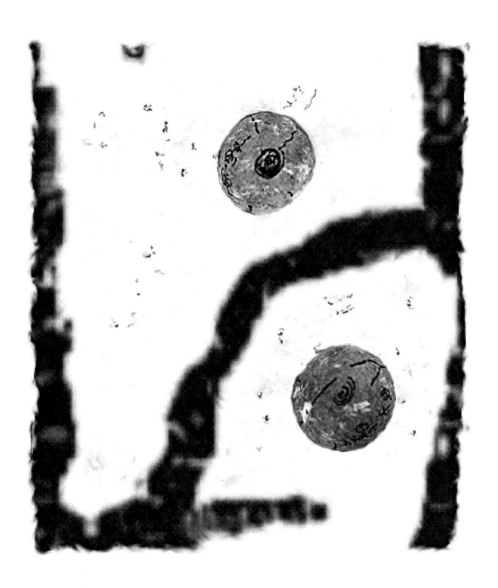

wires grew from the stone,
        heart, and moth wet bursa
   in Neptune's orbit
      whose storms we swam
      tongue-tied, drunk on
viscous infant
         sacs of messiah
      fused into raw metal code

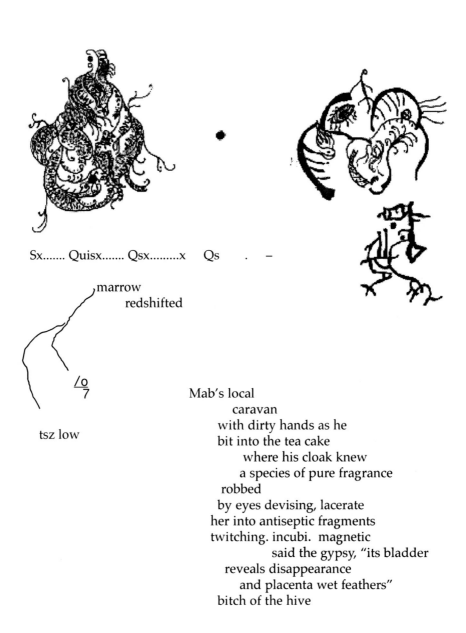

Sx....... Quisx....... Qsx.........x   Qs   .   −

marrow
      redshifted

$\frac{\angle o}{7}$

tsz low

Mab's local
    caravan
  with dirty hands as he
  bit into the tea cake
    where his cloak knew
     a species of pure fragrance
  robbed
  by eyes devising, lacerate
her into antiseptic fragments
twitching. incubi. magnetic
      said the gypsy, "its bladder
   reveals disappearance
    and placenta wet feathers"
  bitch of the hive

bsyh 2 ... sodium radical glamour

she is accompanied by a leopard

———————————— 0 ————————————

I recline in this noble hell
 and pretend an appearance
allows bodies to writhe in warm metal air
      or geography is a world dreaming species through
   Rumi ringdoves singing mercury's
stones to numb muscle sunflower, she
      fuels the nether lamps, pelvis, thistle and yew
            is a solvent parallax
         (flagellants of cypress^2 : to spawn nucleus, Neter-khertet = potentia

      [ignition steel green moonflower
            decides murder in a backseat, handcuffed, dismembered
         transplanted in half countenance
            bartering mandrake for a child
            reverses the corpsewagon

The Castration of Christ
 wailing tombtrains of blue coal
   slept on the tracks and leapt into boxcar
where kneeled in half circle facing the wall
   casting the bones
      "c'mon mama, gimme a 7!"

               or rattlesnake galaxies clustered
                  around milkwhite eggs
               we ripped from the walls of paradise

   1. doves in the distillation train is primary
   2. cross current slag, or ovary jasmine, violate the fecund
   3. aphids suffocated in extraction delete liver and
         indicate the predisposition to flight (inherently lunar)
   4. the infant male afflicted by the bull's device
         requires stratovictus vapor administered as if dreaming
   5. microwave assault foreshadows as an abstract of skull generators
            whose coils devise rust, ideogram
   6. arbor dismembered and scales decalcinated
            pliant to weather and cherub eel
   7. Castor is barren from eye facile bondage
            until the extractor redeems with Quetzal-jade rain

Io succubus light where Padma
   describes her eruptions as the Bowels of the Lord
and ate them metallurgic dogma, plasma's nectarous corruption hung
for
       burlesque assassin in Virgo

          ran her fingers through spilt cognac
          and buried an ear in
               radio –
          & fingers across his phallus till it
            stiffens, bark and sage smoldering
        in glass,   stood naked, painted red
carnelian   drawing figures in the air
horse   while she cradled it between her breasts, waiting –
tumor   fire gnosis
buried in   The dancers collapse
gold   Shiva undone
                in deep static
         barely the waves cohesion –
the ceiling fan knocks through its turns, once each cycle
    bare eyes appear, half-voices in lung memory
              and what sleep leaves
              – thick carpet full of cat piss flesh –
     tongued deliberate to her navel sprouting

broadcasts ligaments   Gate
  through the
  stars   gmn-abl
                cüreuhl drggr
                   imyn
               occulura viscera
                  ...

        assumed
      if negation fathered   [held in acrobat

                languid
             isole
                 pr,..si
     bas   co
              in
              fic
              av
                ient
    al   memnosc
     uob   rotique
        fohr
            shlieb
             ibn-o

out of nothing
the fire quickens, (raids on the arbor.
"They crave that thing. Whatever it may..."
doves scattering
fibrous as confusion   taxi backseat,
zipgun in his boot   miraculously tender
in his criminal spheres
descends through the sloughs of Necropolis (bare limbs through fog) –
Archideus
warmed his hands in assassins and
mockingbird callous, flown from Shekinah
tease the fisherman to
remind his wound
smiling through the cathode at Eden
and the mixed odor,
grass and gasoline

Cain drug her screaming from the pit,
for which he'd trade that Black Wall of blood in the brain,
those horses knew fear too well
to confess a lie in her place, but
suffered the bleak secret sky
for tar in the nostrils and a
razor band of stars that strip the
light from the eye and
name it to death with quadrants and heliotropic despair –
only for pearls against the black breast of Venus
did the documents surrender their deceit
and found her familiar flesh in the tide
and liberal with her pleasures
a horse to ride in violent weather
released from the man shrouded air
clanging the equinox down
singing the equinox down

diamond Jim ain't no center
to lamb these devils their private mirror
80 islands of chaingang gone down
to factory, bleating
Am with heather a constant genus
roped St. Michael to perform ———— Basque prophecies,
dog circus,   who choose themselves alone
an iron cock christened   to retain the neural strain & form
bardic valences roam to meat
between torches of embryo nestled
in thorny euphony
spit roasted by her bachelors,———

but these worlds are obscured
by the savage wrecking media of a day's sound
laid beneath the tongue,
a cherub infection –
Word become venom

In the triangular shape desire
drives its wraiths
to project triple cinema
against their flanks   turned
by a lunar wheel
submerged with debris field scattered
like crows from Chaos Matrix

"Oh mama,
you don't understand, the spine eater
comes with his combines
and thrashing beaks
and I only got this skinbag full of rats to gamble."

:|[but where I am
is only through this device,
though in the original substrate
neither essentially
divides from any other
more than memory is distillate
of measured emergence,
and so knowing these conditions
obstructs plentiful image-flesh grace]|:

faith's passion held in muscle
dark as murder

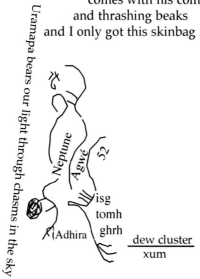

he shot her just as she reached the door
at the height of carnival
when the Golden Ass arrives
bodies interchange,
floods of angels pour from the wound
in pulpy air
bound by their hooves and snouts
saint butchered and sewn

jasmine-crucifer-ring-Math-domain

He went down to himself
length of rope
and lake of sin
listening bone ironies
close enough to shoulder the animal
he'd cleave from absolution

"Nothing's changed.
Did you think a few lightbulbs
and combustion engines could
dispel the hunt?"

Uramapa bears our light through chasms in the sky

carrion
mainline righteous
    scraping his wounds ——
mumbling
mumbling
would not disavow the Lord

down to himself

   – what do you call it?
  – Manhunt.
    brutal as scripture

wringing her hands
"I've got a washerwoman's soul honey.
I've got a brainful of lightning
    ready to blow."

          turning.
In the vitals, just as the liver moved,
by gaping sores
the bees consume

flamed green in the Black Hand

and refused to protest
except mama herself
drawn beneath a perverse discretion
    of vegetable mass

(venom from the root's abundance
    distilled in reservoir phases
    persuading legions to rally
    beneath the somnolent drone
of flies rushing the kill)
    buried
    charred odor of compressed time
    hedged against
    lucifer stars
    clanging the equinox down

chest. revolves.9thgate.heliocentric.sapphire

quark legion
cane vinatici
pupae
amu
drasig
mara

moth dust in absence

nothing eyelash ruse

difficult hearing then
herb bearing ethers

– 99 –

crucifix is embryo
suspended
from phospheme logos –
Sophia ensnared in grinding wheels
of warm lethargy
at the moment of recognition and surrender,
Where the field deposits
from the brink of all luminous spinning variably bountiful,
an accord with infinite
yet numerably substantial
stolen from her mother and bound in animal hides
locked in the trunk
where only a diving bell could restore
a stone graft forged
between transistor icon   strumming cells to habit
nautilus geometry   born in modal Lilith hacking wire

Will follow Mother's doves
to Avernus   (hideous faces)
that stench is memory
drained like flies from my pores
dragging Beelzebub back to his tower of loathing

bodies suspended from a blue sky
remake the eidolon
reweb feverish discourse
until nothing remains but the pelican bleeding her breast for no one

Down to hellmouth
with golden mistletoe
brutally awake
TV extracts flickering plague – draughts of cremation
till the womb releases her waters –
.... –
If soul is vagarious
undulating between universes –
not stars and their antithesis only,   but parallel resonances, or those
abstracted from radiant trails of subtle behavior –
no context could provide the bark
articulation (and who'd die of the weight anyhow)
only unhindered could she consist faithfully   and speak
particles emerge
from 'their' forces shadow
polishing the mount
rider eaten from marrow
electric
rooms…

Infernal darkness has its harmonies
brilliant and unfixed
posturing order from mind too manhandled
these utopias overbear
Saturn to python devouring her moons
rusted in genetic repositories wailing

& a
glowing nonatych
annunciating Salvatore Animal
pandimensional cross-pollinator
who slipped into nowhere laughing

proving his aspect
is paradisal blue bodies in the low branches
in silent observation of anti-ground's

played from Jericho
or Baal erect

spied from orchid hooves
noumenon
planter
round with
arcane clarity
dreamed in begging bowls

their roots unbalanced
are a fricative engine
bred from false dawn circling

raven
bent to fornicate   conned the elliptic

gather for prayer
diminishes
frequent arms,
stratospheric, epiphanous…
.)

whose random powers bear
murdered oblivion

through swollen passages
o

when she laughed
I felt strange beaks

– horse latitudes –
torn screaming neckdeep
twitching vegetable mass
bolted from Jehovah's crowblack
and so
…is the swollen face sold
down to Avernus

iris strangely bleak
repeated
from breasts
delinquented, ominous

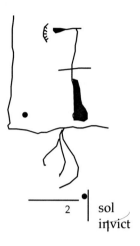

2 | sol
invict

tables of grain
of slaves castrated for revolt
bricks manufactured and shipped
herds broken according to edict
dissolve in amber

"tonight you're
antiseptic lady!"

whores to feed
warm negation
the temple's electrophilic arboretum –
she'd cross Byzantine
cemetery doves
rising from concentric valances
she submitted rather than shave her head

plain of myrrh
suspect and holy
in the senses
… and laid the
moon Sin
run with opal tygers
refined to their essential oils

degrees of sublimity
rain
hybrid
Elohim
beneath eerie first light
bridges crimson until thunder
insinuates eye
from their voices throne
like sheets of steel
tearing

fed livid idols Polyphemos-demiurge-Nobodaddy
arched his back is supper toilet
from healer's red wing shadows 7 worlds
blasted in nectar
drains to anabasis as a moral rite in the oppressor's avarice
tracked them across the lower delta
40 days until gunpowder soaked our blankets
and all scarlet panic of heaven vomited
"let bats carry them away"
slaughtered hogs in the sanctuary
shelved into pirated air
solar flares disrupt
bottles of cartilaginous swarm (throne guards)
fermented,
till she slipped them a 5 to let
bifurcations
describe velocity her clean passage   only   quanta
borne through
transgenous splendor
leapt between orbits

brambu drezi
loca ion
sabayi
sabayi
brambu. isosyn
oua oua oua…
BRAMBU
DREZI
UMGATHAMA

to balance the rivers
crocodile spiked the moss
with distances
notched in mussel shells
beneath mama spider's icon

ochre deposits fertile species
out from nothing
and from that arbor flint sings
lifting the veil, narrowed the channels
only descent between Castor & Pollux, shedding your scales
in implacable darkness
recovers the strain
bison fell nobly
to skull chain rhythm, poured forms from her
voids (her magnetic well,
brown bagged the satyr to stone
in dead motion   bought the nest
bought hegemony whole
and the sockets turned - and lost her thigh to metal -
and sensory web
nations wreck
to prowl the sciences' late viscera
bed of snails near Deneb

Enter Cassiopeia by
dog pack scrounging garbage fossils

covered her in bark, waiting

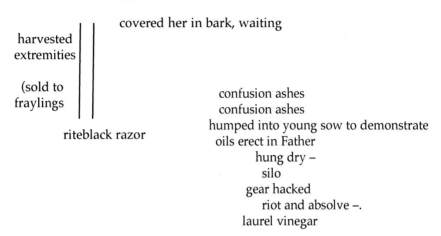

harvested
extremities

(sold to
fraylings

riteblack razor

confusion ashes
confusion ashes
humped into young sow to demonstrate
oils erect in Father
hung dry –
silo
gear hacked
riot and absolve –.
laurel vinegar

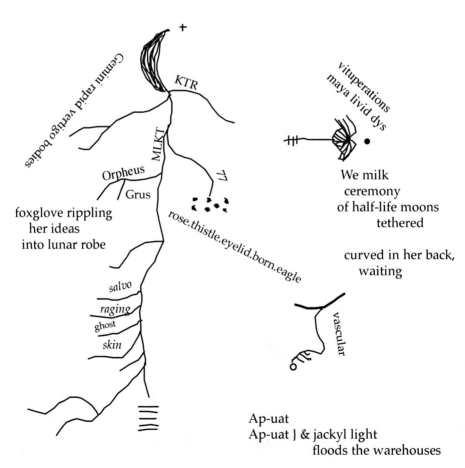

Gemini rapid vertigo bodies

KTR

MLKT

Orpheus

Grus

foxglove rippling
her ideas
into lunar robe

rose.thistle.eyelid.born.eagle

salvo

raging

ghost

skin

vituperations
maya livid dys

We milk
ceremony
of half-life moons
tethered

curved in her back,
waiting

vascular

Ap-uat
Ap-uat } & jackyl light
floods the warehouses

joist. mares gnotting air
                    drawn golem panic storm seizes
                    3 toes

    rifles blue gris demanding
    wheel
        ices the dust   (sweet Christ! these contrary waves)

    funneling
paraclete doves
      dense scattering
        rune engine   ig-ix
                                Floods (Gilgamesh) | random
                                            turret
                                        vapors clone

            gysxk
            canthus
                borrows paradise a fisher's gate
            caught her lust, corn father's burden tied to the ore
        (when Hera was such a frigid bitch)
                Opal fired the gene
                    & pranced through Mary eupany leopard
    drowned in electric congo, from the waist a blue cord sputters

            She was full of pucks
            devising retribution/atonement
        and pristine valences that grant the interrogative
                        "'indeterminate' 'transcends'"
                but gathering this a priori closes nothing
                tames to Black Wall, steals Oblivion's kiss
                        staring through Black Wall
                        staring through Black Wall
        santhgroi im-media   isosyn sabayi
                                UMGATHAMA

            item
        (biers of flight)
            should remain evocative
                gray intestines wing
                smoke in Chac
                    preening river
    50 miles downwind of Regulus
                    boiled in red issue
                threads proto-hybrid
                luscious
            mounted by sparrows storming
                blonde sky
                    – 105 –

Molly Durga

in inverse proportion to control's deceit

[accompanied by a leopard,
which is often Dionysic
joy]

a body of infinite

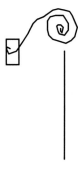

perturbations of subtle air

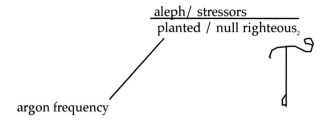
aleph/ stressors
planted / null righteous$_2$

argon frequency

shed her eyes
to gradual reservoir

curses where
sylph tracks in snow
or mistletoe…

robbed by angels
driven south
ashen
red
water faces

Diana's buried face
and white flock

Molly Durga
Molly Durga
who'd feed
chthonic branches
with sweat

clanging

woke with her blood drenched panties in my fist
she who invented orgasm
to check the scorpion in his quarter
and spread across me, ballbox,
till I grabbed her asscheeks
and cast her out,   through the window,
she hit the pavement laughing
(ask Ivan, he saw the whole thing)
air of wet cunt, heresies
familiar chain of skulls swung out from Mars
her secretions soaked the room
the wallpaper sagged and fell to the floor
"It's the damn humidity," he said.

she knows roots
and their electronic ores

grain and plasma serum

xum

eidolon reeds
and a luminous air between

clanging

contraction archs a dual sky
& received them, machine and flesh, to the sea
strega light...   draws nectar
to persuade the corpses' return
isotope oracular

beetles in deadwood
collecting soldiers ————————————

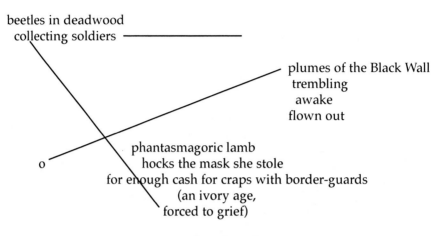

plumes of the Black Wall
trembling
awake
flown out

o

phantasmagoric lamb
hocks the mask she stole
for enough cash for craps with border-guards
(an ivory age,
forced to grief)

... panther claws from memory—.

preyed the radiosacred
leaves its infant
raw diamonds and other trinkets
vats of resin   to scuttle the guilt of predominant face

Exodus —— weeds

thyroid storm
and out you go ————|
.extinguished.

Not a damn thing in transcending
unless piercing absolute, eventually pierces nothing

revolving septenary gate
————————————

dissolves the turning membrane
from her image
boundless to rain

————————————

for Ivan Argüelles

Molly Durga
Molly Durga
found them (demons all) coiled in the bathroom of a 7-11
to get out of the cold
removed her mask   and those hideous scars came to life
torched the eastside for a price
She was down on all four, stark naked, sniffing the rug
"where'd I put my babies,
my sweet little Kataptron and Wüd"

apostles of rubric
apostles of red ochre

"okay, okay, I'll let you in on it
I'm born of Leda and the swan, brother to Helen
and yeah, I humped her once.
Truth is, she loved it, the transgression of it, and conceived by it,
and bore a sickly hermaphrodite
who healed by touch and thought
Lived in a second floor apartment over a bar,
bathed constantly..."
coagulant menses sprinkled on the pruning tools
fuels the mad humming of bees in the hedges
fuels the flame
chain gangs of slaves from the north
spread across the flood plain
snakes in the levee

What could Mother from these seizures?
A wreck of syntax to match the scattered phosphemes —
cardinals gather to feed on the husks—
and the snap peas he left unstrung
or hound cut loose at night
shotgunned with a young sow in his teeth
Oh, they'd wreck the manger for that abomination
But this is no syntax
Or, for that matter a decent harvest —
the seed left for the birds, or to return to the ground all winter
back through Papa Legba
where sugar becomes liquor becomes brown viscous redolence in a clay jar
he grinned and held it to my face, as if to say,
"here, have a snort!"
saw the other, one of many, body
gather the souls fragments
where cardinals feed
where mourners
beg that gray meaty sky to cease

Shekinah, who laid 31
and the 32nd her completion
& vanished there, wet between her legs, to fill the void

going down   her eyes like serpent's
coming up   like emerald fire

You have found the hand in Mu, reordered its profile
old man, face into rock, you know a soundless form

– Why them hounds howling so? Don't nobody ever let 'em hunt
Poised in the underbrush at the edge of the grove
he observes her bent to drink from the stream.
It was an inversion of particulars, though the penalty, and who got it
is accurate. and those hideous scars came to life

For years Chac-Mool wandered among them
in the guise of various genetic maladies,
unable to understand how they could ignore his lamentations –
the new priests seemed utterly dependent on the conjoined
architecture of sound & vision

"Soul is striptease isn't it? With the exception
when you peel away the layers
you're ogling your own nakedness,
and that's nothing baby!"   Deep down in it clawing like mad
until he realized all the parts were alive
and cringing beneath his touch

I dunno how it got there
the lame drag it in
and no, I don't know how
how she got that way

there, among Job's plunder
the serpent finds his
way to the tree

she was scarred,
cut up bad inside
rarely smiled,
her face tragically
void of expression

I wake with someone on top of me,
kissing, or so it seems,
a large mouth   covering mine
I think my wife until
I hear her breathing,
asleep at my side
It's hip is naked and smooth,
soft, female, and it's breathing fast,
hyperventilating reptilian,
but when I open,
focus my eyes — nothing
no one

closed in on the boar –
surrounded,
he turned to face each one in turn
observing death's approach
her erotic strategy.
Circe, why you treat me mean?

Holy of holies, cherub and ark
bark
& leaf

like emerald fire!

UMGATHAMA

rose
heavy

                              sibylline

bathed in   iron passage
     protozoan soup   retreats
                             clings
                             to the smitty

                                   devours

                                             listening to
                                         nerve polyphemia
                                              rising
                                         through vertebrae
                                          & fanning out
                                            across
                                     the skull mind drinks
                                                slavishly

     put the river to bed darling
           time for rest

hermaphrodite grove

          nothing is sufficient
          to merit this lunacy
          sat closed mouth, numb
            following the tribes
                clanging down
                clanging down
            After the dark water's rage
only Yemaya could mirror   (and mirror the void to meet, what polis is this
     that hankers to neon,   rootless
           clanging down

     Tlaloc, darling, will you put the river to bed?

          across the skull
            mind drinks a light

                  lips breach

                  – 111 –

that space is the vault of knowledge
    Tiresias stares the dawn down blind, removes his cloak
  and she is a serpent millennium
      emerging from the wound in his breast, they are beech wood,
        leopard consort of Pan (polished his spurs and brass knucks,
                "Hey Tommy! How much for yr sister?"

        Do I indicate a definite phenomenology? claws in a brick oven,
          pomegranates sewn in your thigh

      "whaddya mean 'let them dogs hunt'? seen Acteon lately?"

"wailing from the grove   "How does one name the holy?"
 in April's recrudescent light,   possess the possessor?
fairies gather around the fallen Christ,   unbabble the fetters?"
cradle his head, its twisted horns…"

   that space is a ferment of equations
     mounted to their familiar,   a finger half in her pushing the wires around
      "I remember the smell of the orchard, musky sweet rot."
   and the wires became souls desperate for an exit, seized the zenia head
         and ripped it from its raven crotch
            as sure as loquacious dead
        Anubis slid along the window sill and froze her with his breath
  to consist faithfully? only if negative able
"hey sis, will ya draw the curtain? they done stole my pants."
his frail body and translucent skin, the multitudes came to him for healing
  and gasped in awe at his aspect, to see God snout deep in the trough
 it is a membrane instinctively worn
to obscure the maker from the made. Such is the
      inceptor of demons and their delight is of no
    small consequence. But a mirror is an imperfect
      familiar at best, and through this fog much
        less so.   bury mirrors, plant the devil
           summon locusts in the gyre
          if polis is body in motion
           tongue-tied doscuri in backwater
          and Baal came tumbling after
           oscillating armpit of the sheep
           wrapped in potassium shell
"There are those that would suggest Qliphoth are the engine of the universe."

oblique salvatore   somber
                  animal
                  bolted
                  shrift
                  repent
                  spinal   & these permutations of the tongues…

Avebenar rm latzed LVC–EKBEVE
naguebcgreba   Jabbok sy notzgu taveroquo
  KOVORK shriteb oenzoh pruiepz
           nuwmua PFQNU veflekvc tedkitx Ivoim boum
   radqupn Qutzdachezl tzolmark
redquwm tefsxo
   ntagm-fgtc bekim-Nov ur-mab-ib naunl
  Tasichzequekel gru lanai BAY–IFA
chv birib Lrin pbovuk
     ocihezahech talethenom izred   Kopitshemeb
   oagoeb onnech grum   germv leti-kamet nesh
        thedlekthtz rebjegury

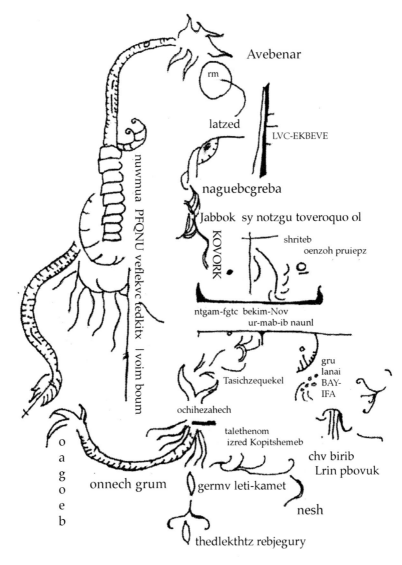

Avebenar

rm

latzed

LVC-EKBEVE

naguebcgreba

Jabbok sy notzgu toveroquo ol

KOVORK

shriteb
oenzoh pruiepz

nuwmua PFQNU veflekvc tedkitx Ivoim boum

ntgam-fgtc bekim-Nov
ur-mab-ib naunl

gru
lanai
BAY-
IFA

Tasichzequekel

ochihezahech

talethenom
izred Kopitshemeb

chv birib
Lrin pbovuk

o
a
g
o
e
b

onnech grum

germv leti-kamet

nesh

thedlekthtz rebjegury

ashes and rain in the Sun's cold harem
　　her dowry forsaken for the head of a lion
　　　　no cesium pulse drags Chronos from his meal
　　　　　and you come up swaggering your pendulous…　　charm
　sheeps skull, ram's bladder, logic board, a bag of ravens thrashing
in the circuitry, a measure of lightning in Orion's sword,
　　these risks I assume are a gate

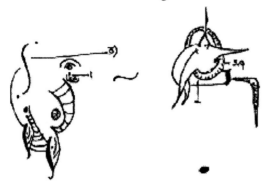

The obituary detailed no
cause of death, but the
medical report said
bloodclot –
an insoluble knot in the heart

telesorium

　　　　purging the grail
　　mastodons awake in the reptile brain, tending their carbon
　　　　flagrant as peacocks in a vase held to Her ear
　mucking around in the corpse, stale oil and diesel bawd salivating
　　　　　　requiem for Christmas
　　　　"Father, father made her brakeman
　　　　　flagging down that indigo line
　　　　　　punch drunk for the riot act
　　　　　　　spat over her shoulder
　　　　　　and saddled the dharma to ride"
　& soft beasts they were, ivory flesh rippling down the canyon
　　through radar convulsion – the nerve sheath of prayer –
　　and a rope of sweet hymen sewn to the eye, paraclete
　　　　purge my ambitions
　　　　drive the locks through swollen death

OBLIVION, BE THE MESSAGE OF MY BLOOD　　　hand in hand
　　　　　　　　　　　　　　　　　　　　　　we descend
　　　　bury Lazarus frothing goat (red-headed
　　　　　child savors the rod),
　　　　　mated the steel or righteous marrow
　　　　in seamless sparrows a gesture of corn,
　　though she'll swallow the beak of Apollo alone
　and run wild through the brambles till her clothes are rags.

she learned to bite her tongue and
not challenge Cain for the soil, but
bear the mark
washed up half alive out of the labyrinth
cochlea drift and Alderberan after with
hyades mourning the boar's rough work
in triple moons
A FUGITIVE AXIS

"these are the furnaces?"

hung himself in his cell
by his pants –
run through jobs,
wives, cash, life.
nothing short of hell
would accomplish its theater,
a blind gesture
taken on the chin — (stares the dawn blind)
Damn.

a large pool of vomit in front of the gate

fingers spread like spokes in a bone riddle of conflict.
they breed rapacious angels, —

the marks along his flank
might be an indication of lean years
not even the old lies
hold their meat in this weather
he digs the hole
where the preserver feeds

deadens the eye an urge
ground to paste in the reeds
or gulf devoured
or plastic iris
and gravediggers extract a menagerie of vital fluids,
wilderness of anesthesia I bargained
for hypospadias, Ashura's secret device,
strode in sanctum machina and pissed the gears raw
(veins are logos an urge

"What we are pursuing is polytemporal. I see your face like a stain
on the policeman's uniform in the harsh florescence of the station,
his fat like a creamy pulp around his face. Not even sleep erases the body."

Eleleth is that you?
Do you know oblivion?
is she virgin? and ripe?

whose
muse
isolates
root and
suffrage
impaled

kindled
hair for

whose muse is solid root and suffrage impaled
swindled Paris for the price of a rite
    who figured the shade for a nom-de-plum
        "that'll get you killed"
    if you can measure the grain against
    energy spent, foot-pounds the lever drew
barges down a dead current, ash & sulphur discharged

        the price of a rite
            who figured the shade for a nom-de-plum
                "that'll get you killed"
            down a dead current,
            draughts of albumen in her face a miracle of

how suffer cunt gladly

messianic ram

messianic ram how suffer cunt gladly mourned in a stupor

        triads; the male habitat frequented b
        hyperphoenician fleets in scales of hook and ox
        and oils whose scent can blind,
        can muster pacts against
            the future's low rape
            laws and dissolute code not flesh enough
        to an eye seething helix
            is blood is ruin
        is screaming a chorus of veins ploughed under
                with corn gone to worms and drought and
    fantasies of syntax no husband could smell on your breath
            torn at the steel-ribbed hell you're naked to swarm
            and feed the frail thieves who carve up your breasts
                    for a mouthful of barbed wire
                    burning through ghost blonde absence

                roses pouring from her mouth

I spoke to her carefully
  at pains not to disturb the glass
    is a dragon   fire
      or lion in white eclipse
    composed of the sun I swallow

        my face a thousand stories deep
      seeded with plagues and amorous beasts
        seized the twin fathers of maelstrom
            and beat her into submission,
        she holds their laws in her teeth
        snapping at the veins
        testing the reins in the stones I hurl
        from a precipice in Jupiter alone

    to bear the mark
    to bear the mark

                        as if time is a cellular dislocation
          I feel the roots in my chest contract
            a conspiracy of laughter in stones I heave
                from zodiac tar
                to bear the mark
                to bear the mark

      is the lion a green sulphur
      freight train penetrating golgotha of Venus –
    I spoke to her carefully
      and she responded, if at all, with barbed vacancy
    and the air around her crackled   reduced to raw –
        her paws in stone, her antlers discharge taloned salvos
                        across the Red Sea
                        in my veins
    is this 2nd nigredo Damballah's convergence,
    Alba Melanos?

              in the White Darkness
              Be my rider,
            when there is nothing left of me
              Be my rider

              Be my rider
              Be my rider…

a tooth of fire
spoke like graves breathing

amul
eah
yu
oua
coh
sah
ri
iheo
ou

Herü gone to earth
crashed against the kitchen window
the imprint of barbed axions
across the sulphur pit of
solstice noon coiled

beneath a
kosmos: boiling faces,

Nova Cygni   the
crucifer egg   x-ray panopolis
dabbled in witchcraft
taking license with a stunned hawk

a
u
o
a
o
r
u
a
u
o
a

across
yesod familiars the
whirling bride
Dolphy swung outward bound
Horses run out of
the meaty infinite
the python ripe with lambs

scattered along the embankment
collected by trawlers
drunk and wenching the
river primary Enoch in
north Anatolia, felt hat
and cane tucked his wings in the
cranial morass that looms the world
from topheavy trees Molly Durga gone
down to harvest
teats swollen red

brief fixtures to lance
their fraudulent claims   the dead mount
parabolic as desire is thorns
wound into vapor
all species a bare suspension

5 naked arms
grown from the wheel
tangled masses of hair, nail polish
requiem and fossil
tangled hybrid gyroscope

tangled hybrid

that "*And* " before is an ontic
Hinge

from which hangs   from which swings —
... dys-c(h)ord   "darkness opened
oblivion, still
a   dys-c(h)ord all
genesis buys
in the   senses
("apprehension")
uncoiling
to feed the brain
a seizure in flower

see, we bring food to the ancestors
propped in "fetal" con:
elaborate morphogeist
with anarchist tendencies
scattered to Chac or some other
chronometer rot

sealed but nourished in fungal episodes

a thigh
erect and polished

th... cl... r.te .... ld...ss of...

2
3
7
7
4
9
-
-
-
|
6
9
7
+
.
.
.

"profusion" or seething light
                    visceral damp (Abulafia's animal)
          was that her fur?
     where entelechy is a bursting corpse?
       when late afternoon sun
       slid away like a quilt
         and the revealed abyss erupted electric fangs
                              and honied tongue
       and a flurry of magpies
     descend on the body's familiar weight?

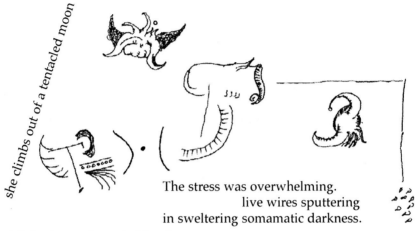

she climbs out of a tentacled moon

The stress was overwhelming.
          live wires sputtering
     in sweltering somamatic darkness.

I fight the tendency in blood
to slow the fuse
  — draughts of entropy
     — a mask in the desert shouting the names
  — the serpent who feeds at my navel
  ravenous for the silences
Salvatore Animal,
  brass accident of YHVH's bargain

"Oh yeah?" "Well take your 2-door red convertible attitude and go fuck yr fist!"
          Nergal daysin Dirge!

crimes in the nursery   Artaud drove the howlers out

          "So then, body is columnar motion,
          beast vomit in time, and a rotten gate at that.
          What we assume is the venerable pleasure
          of our damnation and we're made holy by it.
           A congregation is called by passion's debris;
          the devils sniff around it, lick its eyes
          and chase the moths that die in
           its lashes, and this apprehension is a devouring
          that drives Chaos."

or Golden Ass porking Mary, just so much
bait thrown to the gulls
drums reckon in solid waves among the noble gases
stalking green Sodom, fell in his chair to plea the bartab
from Sophia righteous enough
runs the gate raw pissing

hybrid elementals

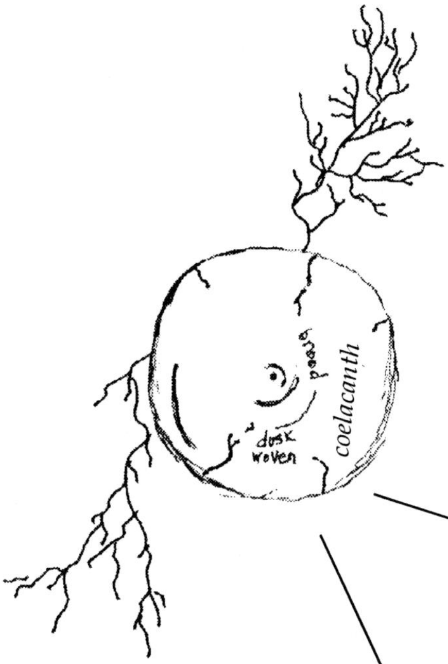

alternate chambers
stripped from projection
cypress is flame

coelacanth
creed
dusk
woven

chosen
humid renders flesh

dance affirm fuel
preyed on the distances
tapped from mollusk
wet husk and cock, swung
from the rail laughing
scarlet trains of sea bass
out of sweet nowhere running
to that jukebox murmur
down the hall out of sight
wet as her thighs are

drained oracular

coagula vox

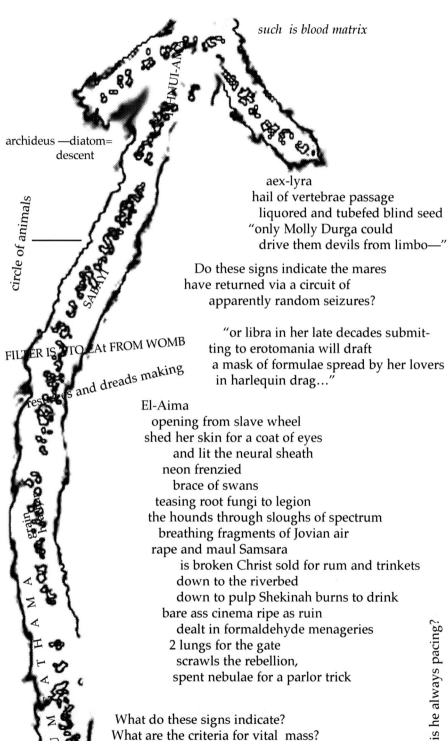

such is blood matrix

archideus —diatom=
descent

circle of animals
_____

aex-lyra
hail of vertebrae passage
liquored and tubefed blind seed
"only Molly Durga could
drive them devils from limbo—"

Do these signs indicate the mares
have returned via a circuit of
apparently random seizures?

"or libra in her late decades submit-
ting to erotomania will draft
a mask of formulae spread by her lovers
in harlequin drag..."

El-Aima
opening from slave wheel
shed her skin for a coat of eyes
and lit the neural sheath
neon frenzied
brace of swans
teasing root fungi to legion
the hounds through sloughs of spectrum
breathing fragments of Jovian air
rape and maul Samsara
is broken Christ sold for rum and trinkets
down to the riverbed
down to pulp Shekinah burns to drink
bare ass cinema ripe as ruin
dealt in formaldehyde menageries
2 lungs for the gate
scrawls the rebellion,
spent nebulae for a parlor trick

What do these signs indicate?
What are the criteria for vital mass?
poison in waves

why is he always pacing?

dance from impossible anthrophtera
dance to oblivion and her 3-headed sister
"trade his cum for a roof and half a glass
of the lamb"
dance to Mare Oblivion
torn from the sky
torn from the grove
every muscle in her thigh strains to articulate
concoctions of the void struck
in resinous hives
infused with spines boiling faces,
blue desperate bodies

caught in the
outnoise dancing blood toward

CODA: CYGNUS WOUND

Are there bones here?
Or merely a name,
an abstraction smothered in grotesque mirrors –
slices of human thigh,
emerging from the black distance,
wagons in paradisic unreal landscapes of the virgin west,
carrying the corpses further –
mounting her like a great mare,
Legba opens the way –
her eyes are blank white, flame,   cigar and shades,
tongue-tied deathless eloquent,
her hair tied back in long braids
These hot afternoons summon the revelry of night
serpent on a crucifix,
jewels and fragments of dream down that long white abyss
Nightingale screams,
"Get off that barbed wire boy!
it'll take the balls right off you! make you
a better catholic than yr mama's prayers intended."
(castration as consequence of devotion,
Attis, Ceres, Adonis)

gone down in the drink,
drug his daughter to safety before the current took him –
My last fair deal gone down, good Lord,
She was just a plaything to him,
she kisses the swan's head as he rapes her
Last fair deal gone down –
"and when his wife found out about it, good Lord,
well, like I said, that was the end of it,
till those damn x-rays confessed her grave."

dance to refrains of the infinite curvature of space
my fingers crowded with
"worlds to come",
sucked from gladiolas at river's edge, at Time's charred horizon.
The banker's fumble with their frocks and lucubrations
grass in their teeth
gone Nebuchadnezzar mad
(the tablets were primarily accounts of agricultural exchange
the priests' stock dwindling in favor of the military court)
execution style,
the barrel, usually of a handgun, is placed at the back of the skull where the
spine flowers in brain; death is sudden, "out it blows".
Who will speak for the dead in heaven?

dance to impossible Anthroptera
dance to Oblivion and her
3-headed sister

"he made and signified these things"
or Orpheus hung in Hades forever –
& his lyre beside him, overhead now in the summer constellations,
is that the pit of hell?
drink deeply and the land is healed, but suddenly darling
your face has changed, you seem older somehow
How can the void be said to have a source?
Thunder in the mountains, rain in the desert, the egg ready to hatch –
What, by inverse proportions, appears to be a bifurcation of the event;
one might appear in several places simultaneously.
her head was throbbing now, her features
distorted by the pain, her memory retreating,
Have you seen the women in Jerusalem
mourning for Tammuz?
you will see things more detestable still!
god lends Manhattan a tiny firmament
tragic as lambstragic as lambs
as reeds in the sun name their talisman,
erect,
a chain of faces through memory's long glass tube
are shackles that turn the soul
perpetually eastward
until entropy rots the circle
a seed in the nerve net –
these limbs bear the names I trace in dust
at Loma Preata they're still talking about the quake,
what happened there?
An acrobat is a salamander
is the smell of sheets the
morning after
is a palm pressed against the window pane
and long screams behind
The room began to fold and splinter
for a second I was lost,
she was smiling at me,
she was lying through her teeth
"They're more likely to appear
in the cold dry months when the air is thin,
when the veil is thin."

The river breaks your fingers
with a lightning storm so fierce
you change your notions of the double natured beast

swung from a cross
    still ravenous and raving for the meat in Time,
  a constant dream in Aristotle's wet fist
  gone to the river
  gas mask in hand
Lord help me mama, I need a razor
  and 6 mirrors in the devil's toy box
  I'm in a fever for light
    and I've gone where the nymphs can't lead
  to feed on parasites
    ghost beyond ghost beyond ghost
  "words are just dead ideas rotting"
(a personality displaced,
    consumed by its own translucence)

We can no longer separate the stars
 or the currents in the navel of Hades
or Sadir, the breast,
    rising and falling in the swelling dark
 the kabbalists name Daath —
  no sky at all, but pure unbroken light
 the stars so compressed and alien
and the switchboard constantly nagging for attention
 " Will someone please get the damn phone?"
  what do these salesmen desire
  but to rob the cruxpoint of its heat,
caught themselves in the dragon's maw
  that points north and from there gathering the cups and uneaten cake
  the hungry traffic silence
(the pain one must bear to be comfortable in this world is enormous)
    here, a cafe buried in infinite daylight
      is a vibrant cancer here at the bottom of the well,
 We can no longer separate the clanging stars.

    We begin.
    The dream has murdered the dreamer
      with a key of tongues,
  her fingers manipulating the seabed,
   and the necklace between her breasts sobbing,
    12 trees in the wound,
    thunder in the west,
    I study the heart of Brahma
      and hear voices
 when they tore her from the tree
  the branches sighed,
    down at the crossroads, down at the crossroads
    they say he comes smelling of graves.

hey Papa, please let me pass
see, I bring sweet tobacco
            and doves for stew
bury her heart beneath the roses
her eyes beneath the Oak
and she will rise again someday
he wrote until dawn and received the third baptism of Spirit,
        he clutched the adversary's thigh, and refused to
release his hold,
            for a name, for a deal in blood,
        to bear the mark
        to bear the mark
                    out of nothing

                            a fire

BRAMBU DREZI
Book Three

for Hank Lazer, Jon Berry, and Wayne Sides

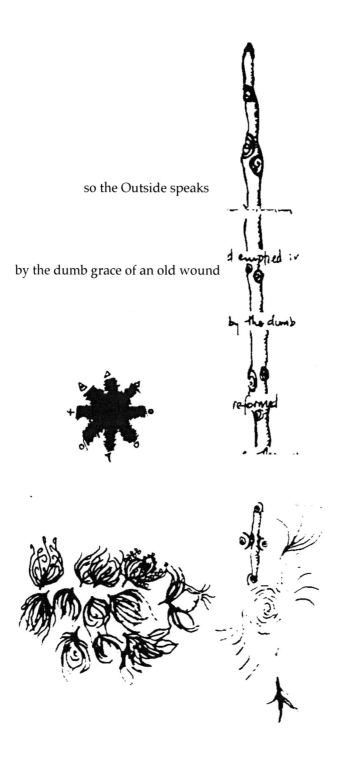

so the Outside speaks

by the dumb grace of an old wound

"Here we go through the edge
and out into the empty."

cacophony, dust, desperation

In the clutch of blind embryo
madness is a tongue robbing death
in the matted black hair of darkness —
I read its invisible shapes
I feel the cold horse thicken and warm and open
in the throes of its engine
and taste the stench of his nostrils
like a prophetic salt
that sweetens the spleen with ash winged moths
that scatter the eyes like well oiled weapons
into the spinal pits of Gan Eden —

his shoulder is worn raw and broad
as the scalloped wings of the Mississippi delta,
his lichen is dosed in meticulous parasites
that will tax the merchant fornicators
(wasn't the abortion of polis built in from the outset?)

I am drunk old pony
on your sweat and exhalations
I am drinking your neck and brow
as we penetrate this matted Night whose violent empty wheel
drove the old women from their ploughs
to denizen horsefly demons in mating caves
that pock the ocean's bones
In its chambered vortex of knots
the Destroyed acquires an insatiable rhythm
and sinks his ax into the soft swan belly
of the infant that lives in my brain and sets my skull on fire
overwhelmed in this spiralling jet of ancestors
that seize the levees and drag them
back to the mountains and drag the mountains into the abyss.
Their pulsing flesh-blue figures dominate
the boundless sky that lies between the vertebrae
whose long electric veins
pour an ape and angel into old winds and hollows.
(he is invincible, serene and dialectically insane ABA / AMA —

But I run my horse deeper toward the open desert
toward a thin brown man, his gold helmet shinning
summons a fish swarm from the sand
with orange sheets of fins full of green suckling mouths
And old man Crow crouched in the bush
and a thick fog played across his eyes
and he thought he saw figures in the mist
dancing with his daughter, dancing with his daughter
born too late from the feathered horn
born too late and never born

she falls at dawn through the wet air
    in a quilt of livid roses —
                her breath smells like infinity rising —
and turns the key in the mollusk gates beyond Saturn
    where skin is a measure against your shadow
    and your shadow is the remainder of bodies that slipped
one from another like leaves dripping centuries
    into a pear shaped goblet the serpents drink to remember —
Their jungle is a sweltering secret
     written in the agony they plant in the veins of a stranger
  who loses his nerve in the face of an unformed god
sweating and heaving and trailing intestines
  strewn in 12 currents that shape the eyes
    you read in a cruel black cup of coffee

    come closer and speak to the dead ones
    speak to the dead who lie still and never cease to move
     by their worms, by their fantasies deleted
     when the mirror burst and its fires flew out
    beyond the heavy elements —

    "Am I leaving now? I feel as if I were dreaming and…"
    "Lie still a while and listen,
            agony is prelude,
      It is only the impossible that lives."

    When he was in bed, waking up or lying down to rest
    with the house quiet, that was the only time he was truly
    alone. He could think if he wished, but the constant
    burn of his thoughts, that odor of charred wire and
    circuitry from inside his head, made thought so
    unappealing that he usually dismissed it and lay there
    listening inside himself, still as the ground, hearing
    nothing, insensate…

2 horns rising over black fur
over that black weight she carries in her eyes
A train traveling North
    and beyond that the names have no
    consequence, no relation

    2 horns rising over black fur
     holding power long enough to mark the ceremony she makes
    hiding her rings in a scarf she tucks into her pillow case
        before she goes to sleep.
      The land ends. The tracks run out.
    A white boat full of flowers is taken out by the tide.

  "Years ago, late at night, one of the local radio stations played classical
    music, but the broadcast originated somewhere else. The sound
    was lousy, as if it were coming through a muted valve, but precisely
    because of its inferior quality it created a kind of spell, an
    enchantment, an invocation of distance. Someone, at some remote
    location was selecting the music, playing it, but even there I think
    the music felt distant, removed, astonishing, empty."

        The land ends.   roads disappear.
  The birds separate from their shadows.
    "You sat by the mirror in the gray early light, no longer human, lost
    in the waves of gravity that licked your shoulders and beat in your
    ears and spread you so thin the cold air took you."

      The field becomes oblivion when I speak it
          the wheels in the waves
       lights in boiling oil
        I try to speak and the words slip through my lips
      before my tongue can place them
       The field becomes oblivion
      when branches clutter the grass and
       starlings burn as they fly through hourglass labyrinths –
       lust is a hymn in the muscle and cartilage
        forbidden in eternity
            12 angels emerging from a cicada husk
       light on the storm's edge
         and all these fiery cadavers singing

opened the immaculate face

I can see them in the twilight rising
   the houses slip into their power
 and shudder into ghost towns,
      & their half-lit mothers unbuckle their skins and
let fly all the soul generations plant
   across rude wet midnight nipples,
 drown their mutations in gasoline to
   worship this sex and vanity
 sucking sublime from the hooves and stones
   and birch bark canoes

AMA
_____

the red issue of Marah

my love will come to me
from out of the corpse I made
   shimmering in the seditious wind
polished by the sand
      crawling through the barricades

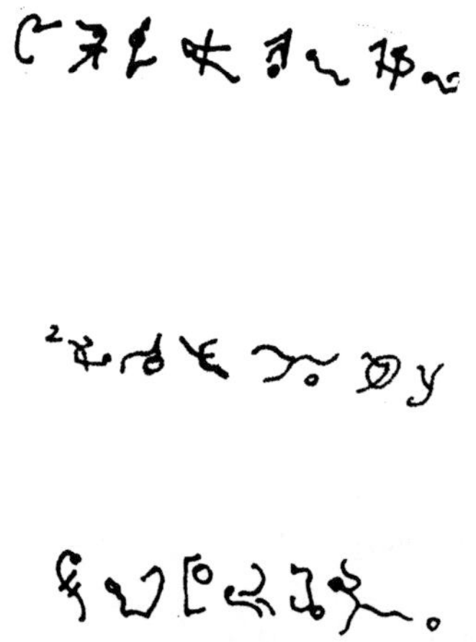

and reckons from my smouldering skull

a liquid code

the trees are full of voices

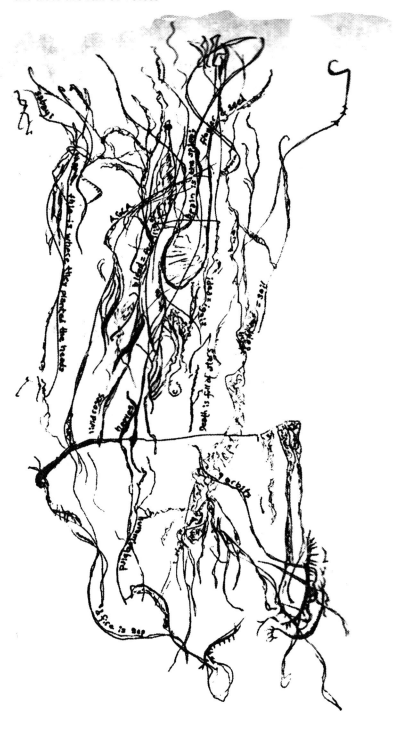

the trees are on fire

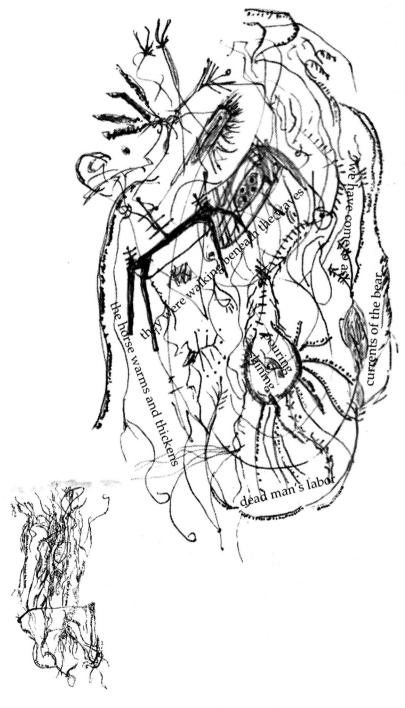

they were waking beneath the waves

we have come to ask

currents of the bear

the horse warms and thickens

pouring shining

dead man's labor

Three days into the mountains the old man set off north to scout a trail he thought might lead to a lower pass. By the next morning he still had not returned so two of the boys followed the trail to a point where it began to break. For the rest of the day they searched the surrounding woods and hills, but nothing, no sign of him, living or dead.

We drink wilderness.

Finally the pain overcame him and he fainted. When he woke it was past midnight. The house was silent and dark except for a lamp burning in a room he'd forgotten. He sat up and tried to make his eyes focus on the room, to force his memory to respond to an image that had no residence there. Nothing. As far as he could recall this room had not been there before he fainted. Now, obviously as his eyes saw it, in a house he'd lived in for most of a decade, and perhaps as a result of his fainting, a new room had appeared; a room that was the only source of light in the house. His heart began to beat heavier, in rapid flurries, sweat broke out over his brow. Something impossible was happening and he sat helpless in its full assault. Gradually he gained enough courage to rise to his feet. Slowly he began to move through the dark house toward the room, toward the lamp. After several long minutes he came to the threshold of the door of the room, his heart pounding, his head throbbing with fear, his eyes watering, struggling against disbelief, trying to balance knowledge and appearance. Inside, the lamp sat on a small table that was situated against the wall to the right of the door. There on the table as well were two yellow pears, a glass of clear liquid he took to be water, an ink pen and a few sheets of writing paper. To the left of the doorway, across from the table and filling most of what he could now see was a small plain room was a large bed with high posts at the corners that terminated in wooden globes. There was nothing else in the room except a chair at the table and a large crucifix that hung on the wall over the bed. After a long while he stepped into the room and went to stand over the table. He lifted one of the pears, sniffed it, studied it for a moment then replaced it exactly where he'd found it. Just as he did this he was struck with the certainty of what he must do. Amidst his bewilderment he wondered where this certainty came from, but it was there, compelling him, offering no other option. It was the only action possible, the reason the room had appeared and why he'd risen from his faint, as if summoned, to discover it. Without hesitation he stepped back across the room and closed the door so that he was shut inside. Then he returned to the table, pulled out the chair and sat down. He took up the pen, turned toward the bed and waited.

I came here to speak of the gathering dead
  in the smell of singed hair
in the songs the dead sing in their bodies
  when breath is no longer possible
and the ghost cannot fly –
    I came here to speak of the dew colored leopard
that circles them as they pass
    between posts that rise
on either side of a river that floods
    when the slaughtering game begins –
    I came here to disavow the electronic haze of eternity
    that saturates our eyelids
when we corrupt our animal silence
  and wear blindness like a skin
  offering cold meat to the close night breathing –
I came here to sing from out of the river's mouth,
  to brood in those impenetrable waters,
  so deep into the green turbulence that I drink an
occult maelstrom of faces, warped and lost from their skulls
    half eaten by the faceless creatures here but still alive
    in some recess the mind invents to deny
            the pure truth of its terror –
I came here to speak of the gathering dead
    and study with my lips the mouths that assume
    the shape of the vacuum they leave
    tumbling through the wound and tumbling
    out a voice that vanishes as soon as it sounds —
In her arms I'm more afraid, wrapped in moist bark, feeling
  my claws and ribs and teeth

And that melancholy door made of shadows
  that revolt against their makers
    brings the distorted beasts home to me, tethered and foaming
  run clear of the mirror raped with nightingales
screaming blue pockets of ammonia as they explode into the glass
    when the night nerves opened, when the castrated earth
  bellowed into the suburbs an old woman's hands shook at her fruit
and loosened the muzzle of the righteous while they ran
  devouring the graveyards, stealing eggs from the laboratories
in Mama's quivering abdomen –
      her stamen machine is a twisting drill
    thick in the ticking that comforts pathogen lunations
  where I sing beaten and broken to sleep

open the gravedigger's mouth
with a song for each of the bodies he's known
open the ribcage and the white wings spread
as the great bird begins her ascent

I am more stark and savage
   that any cell Time imposes
or this ghost train of malignant stars
 that pass through me
like flashlight men scattering rats.
 Ain't no self in here.
 Ain't no empty shell.

my eyes spread out in sunyata tears
   the sky boils out of blue vagina
         cool against another sun in the swamps in
another fierce world
   where we suffocate and stumble out of herds full
of devils,
   jackals in the sweltering heat —
There is no law but lust and obsession and
   the sudden collapse in silent oblivion
   that trembles and calls the forms to life
      with a tongue bent into the folded flower
      of a loa that longs to be sung

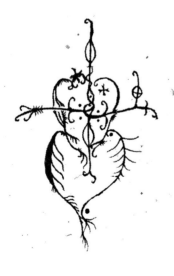

Papa forgive me for my long absence
I have stripped the valley of daylight
   and her hearses
   and erased the arbors
 and scattered the factories,
   You are uncontainable
   So we read in the shards
         of your broken vessels
   a spectral gospel fractured with miracles
      The river is uncoiled
         by plagues of light
   The birds have learned to love falling
and drive the earth apart
   from the hinges of sewers

I am absolved in being
 but I am imprecise
I could be anything
      and still unaware that I am dead—
      beneath the hunter's gaze on sharp hooves
      or stealing across the face of the moon
      with a belly full of rain

landscapes

Eerie red twilight.
Thunder in the north.
Wind claws at the eaves,
    windows and doors..
"the jade fungus of immortality"

The stars disappear
sun eater
lightning in water

10 wells
scattered across the countryside.
figures in metal
    voids in the clay

& beyond that
all the spiralling events
  of the glowing animal writ large

The force of the seizure woke him. It shattered his will and tore at his insides. It destroyed the capacity of his soul to waver, as it often had in youth without intending, between the multitude of worlds. For days he lay in his coffin hardly aware of what had happened. The islands had been broken into long streams then separated from one another by grotesque barriers made of fish intestine. The stench was unnerving.

Men who had been perfectly stable before suddenly became enraged. They took knives or stones or whatever lay at hand and brutalized the first person they met in the street. The truly introverted were driven further inside and thus initiated a self-destructive revolt.

Such destruction is primarily invisible, at least initially, since the individual is attacking himself so deeply within that he alone is aware of the damage. And he may delude himself as to the origin of his pain. He might wake one morning with the uneasy feeling of being tortured, but he has no idea from where or by whom. At this point the imagination projects men with bloody cudgels dancing around a large fire, and sees the slaughtered lamb hanging from a branch in the shadows. Immediately he assumes these to be his tormentors, though he has no idea why he would draw such an absurd conclusion. Perhaps it is because just at that moment they seem more real to him than his own hands and arms. All the faces with their murderous intensity, painted in ochres and blood seem so certain and infallible that he trusts them implicitly. "What could they intend by my murder?" he asks himself, then feels ridiculous in the face of the question. Still, he feels somehow the unwilling victim of their ceremonies. For a few minutes he falls asleep, a sweet dreamless oblivion, but shortly finds himself staring into the roaring flames, mesmerized, waiting.

People see him at work or at public functions and notice he seems to be preoccupied, but when they confront him about it, he apologizes and says he hasn't been sleeping well. Indeed, he is almost as ignorant of his affliction as they are. Day in and day out the dancers continue and their chanting grows louder. He hears them speaking to him in the machinery at his job or in the car engines on the highway. It is as if they are shouting at him by the thousands to lie down, take the elixir and surrender.

Eventually, and no one knows quite when, he is so dominated by the internal hordes that he strikes out at them. He drives his fist through every mirror in the house. Between the rooms he leaves long trails of blood running from mirror to mirror in a desperate attempt to defend himself against his persecutors.

So the coffin holds many secrets and waking is even more perilous. At least when buried one attains a kind of independence from the world; the world of the past, and from the present since one is hopelessly unoccupied. And of course one is not buried at all. The process continues. The sun rises, one showers and goes to work as before, but an independence of expectation, especially one's own expectations remains. From this independence springs a hopefulness that makes the return inevitable. But return to what? Memory is useless because it is only the record of events in a domain that has been rendered insignificant through the event of a grave. And memory is easily shattered, the fragments tumbling in blank ungravitied space, shapeless and no longer resembling the life that spawned them. So one does not return so much as recover some vital impetus and learn to breathe again. Certain assumptions have to be made if one is to begin, so one projects from that basis and pretends a quiet confidence. Laughter comes less easily than before (or so the assumptions would indicate) and carries in its tones a solemn weight and distrust of any impulse that would result in laughter. Even walking carries a measure of difficulty. Any action at all is a transgression against that still perfection of the tomb, the seed of everything that follows. Faces are much more honest however. They are obviously the very shape and beauty of well tended deceit. The entire fabric of existence is fabricated whole cloth from these coolly orchestrated deceptions.

He waited for the car to disappear, watching the
tail lights fade down the street, beneath the long rows
of trees, leafless now in the winter rain. Hands
in coat pockets, collar pulled up beneath his chin.
"What am I waiting for? She's gone. It's damn cold."
He mounted the last few steps to the door, turned,
despite himself, took one last look down the street,
and stepped inside.

"So you met."

"Um-hm."

"And you were married shortly afterward?"

"Mm – no, not right away. We used to spend hours on the phone. At that time he worked on the river, on a boat, pushing barges. He was up all night, keeping watch, so he was lonely. He'd call and I'd keep him company till daylight."

"What do you mean he was 'keeping watch'?

"For debris. Rocks, large limbs and trees that might get caught in the current, maybe wash up under the barge, or get caught in the machinery. They might lose a day or even
a week to repairs if they weren't careful."

"I see. So you became better acquainted during these long conversations?"

"Oh, yes. You have to talk about something. You tell all the old stories and jokes you know, inevitably you get into personal history. Before long you've confessed your great sins, every dirty trick, you fall in love."

"Out of vulnerability?"

"Out of exhaustion. It's all that's left, your resources are depleted. There was nothing left of me. I grabbed hold where I could."

"This sounds more like desperation that love."

"Do you really think there's a difference? Everyone I ever knew that was in love, really in, was completely desperate."

"At this point you married?"

"Yes, out of a survival instinct. Not that either one of us could survive, but our collaborative routine, our emptying one another."

"But obviously something remained?"

"Nothing remained… except the habit of fear."

"And that was enough?"

"You have the facts in front of you. Draw your own conclusions."

For months we worked through official channels,
   but found no one in the bureaucracy sympathetic.
How does love between an impoverished servant
and a foreigner compete with the removal of mountains,
   month long floods that alter a river's course forever?
   So gradually we made the acquaintance of smugglers,
   black market arms dealers, merchants of the skin trade.
   "The factories bombed to ruin
   and resources dried up anyway,
The embargo – the backroom deals between the suits and royalty,
   everything in the shipping channels blown out of the water.
   Some of them leaked so bad they sunk in port. None of them
stocked weapons except the pitiful rifles the troops carried.
   During one attack we were too close coming in –
   after the battle we went up on deck, the
     water had turned to blood all around us
   trailing off toward the western horizon."

He is warm and scaly
 and bristles at my touch
  and sick of lying here in the damp
waiting for a spring that seems
 to slip away breath by breath.
  The small teapot on my desk
  the serene patina of age –
   Earth becomes air
  air becomes earth, then the rain
   owl feathers
    flood
  tamarind, cinnamon & red clay dust
  ruby colored sheets scented with musk
  the vertebrae chain
  black animal cloud swirling
   then a storm in the desert
   and a river of bloodlust
  Hölderlin, out of madness coaxed
  the modern
  which is all madness
exhales when I speak to her half asleep
 wrapt against my chest
 "What is your name?"
 (may those that are bound in heaven
   be cut loose with the flames)
I was too startled to answer,
 but when the voice asked again I said,
"My name is No One. All I can tell you is
 the old man has always called me No One."

A giant rises out of the clouds and shakes his fists at the sun.

The voice did not respond, but I
heard sounds in the darkness like the rustling of leaves,
   like heavy drapes blown around by the wind – but there were no leaves,
   no drapes, and no wind. I reached for the lamp.
 Then I was waking up on the cold stone floor, it was morning,
  the old man was leaning over me, "What's the matter No One, did
     your dreams toss you out of bed?"
  I felt as if he were speaking to someone else.

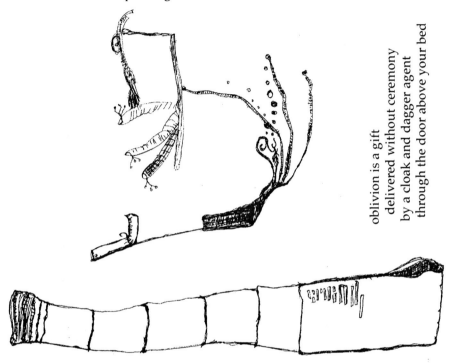

oblivion is a gift
delivered without ceremony
by a cloak and dagger agent
through the door above your bed

          sorry I made the tea too strong
          I should have used the wooden spoon
            There are features of the sky I cannot explain
                    with words or photographs
            The broken boards in the fence
              that runs on top the high red wall
            the amber late November sunrise
          a clear pool gone black & covered with yellow leaves –
            all of them figure into the water in your cup
         the same way a sheaf of cypress branches transmute the music
                 you will be listening to
            some morning, standing at the foot of the stairs
          leaned against the sunroom window,
               waiting for the car to arrive
        that takes you to a wedding from which you won't return
               inside the skin you'll long remember
               from a time "before the war"

The tales they told were embattled rites:
   a lock of hair that disappears among the yellow leaves,
the wind inside her torn silk sleeve, her
     long white scarf lost among the stones and waves,
   drifting in the current like a strange sea weed,
Songs of departure, barely remembered melodies –
A soldier, home at last, has a baby in his arms,
   his eyes are red with tears. He is told,
or overhears, that she has gone into the mountains –
   but nothing is found along the trails, in the caves
or mountain villages, not even a shadow.
    "They say there is
     A still pool even in the middle of
     The rushing whirlpool –"
   or ghosts that move like drops of ink in a bowl of water
   or a charred page from the book he was
    reading before the fire.
   The horses are left to graze all night,
    the early morning traffic sounds like wind,
   even the quail stop singing long enough
    for the sun to rise.
  Large white garbage trucks come Tuesday mornings
   and unload the noisy men who took away the
last photographs of my brother in full uniform.
There are always wars, and the dead return unnamed
   with holes in their chests or their faces erased
but this was our war and there was no one to fight.
Over the horizon the arrogant specters of our past advance
   with all that passion and nothing to loose.
We sat there, huddled in the desert, armed to the teeth,
  waiting – The food was awful, there was no place to shit,
the sand got inside your clothes –
   but your absence hasn't left me bitter, here among these
   mountain folk I am trying to remember
   the smell of your skin when you came out of the bath
While a faceless man pours rice through his flute
   and plays to ease a young woman's labor.
   Still, I don't remember.
I am silent most of the time – and I wait.

How long can a reflection or a shadow last?

Twenty-three days and nine months out, just before noon, the eclipse began, for an hour we were captives of the black sun –. At full eclipse the birds stopped singing and the sun became a great glowing hole in the sky. One almost expected the mountains and rivers, trees, houses and people to be sucked into its vortex and go swirling into the hole.

Later we heard that one of the hermits that lives in the hills outside of town had seen much more – long processions of anomalous animals rising toward the sun, leopards with wings like bats, insects as large as a camel, monstrous serpents wrapped around their legs, and other beasts impossible to describe. And out of the hole poured a column of milk that sprayed across the southern sky in egg shaped drops that became fireflies above the cemetery. These, he said, were the souls of the dead returning.

I was left speechless by the news. Could she mean the storm had destroyed everything in town north of the railroad? Would I return in ten years a rank stranger, unable to recognize my own street?

"How are you Maria?" She'd left the door open, I could hear everything. "Is he here? I heard he was back. I'm eager to see him."
"Yes, come in, he's here, but he's not himself at all. He's irritated by anything I say or do. He goes for hours, sullen and totally silent. He walks around the house aimlessly. I think I heard him muttering to himself. And he sleeps half the day. At night he paces in the backyard, looking up at the sky. I understand there was a storm, perhaps that has something to do with it."
Whether some of them were spies has been a matter of debate for many years now. On one hand, there are accounts of atrocities – whole families killed in their beds so quietly and suddenly that some of them seemed peacefully asleep until you noticed the wounds. On the other hand, none of these stories have been reported by credible first hand witnesses. It is quite possible these rumors were spread by the government in an effort to generate public support for eliminating the sect entirely.

Nothing changes.
children are dragged to the bathtub
and drowned by their mother,
a young rabbit feels the
wind from the owl's wings,
then nothing.   A shot is reported,
the police find a gun on the floor but
no body, no blood, no sign of struggle.

Ten days after the eclipse, just before dawn, the earth shook violently, graves
were ripped open. Later, when men from town went to investigate, they
discovered all the bodies were missing. Not a single bone to be found. The
only person known to be awake at that hour in the vicinity was one of the
komuso who frequently played the flute before sunrise. But he too was
missing, and since no one knew his name, or had ever seen his face, he was
impossible to trace.

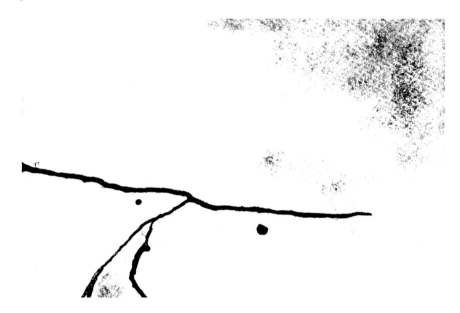

11.24

nothing remains
but a few leaves in the highest limbs
and a large bare branch
peering out of its lone
whale eye   unblinking

The men carried her body toward the burial mound
wrapped in a silk shroud printed in beetles and dragonflies
   The scribes followed holding a wall of mirrors
      that told the story backwards while the children listened –
   long braids were wound
            around her shoulders by trembling chambermaids
who feared look her in the face
            or gaze too long at her reflection —
and the terrible days came, rain beat holes in the roof
   till eunuchs were sent to patch them,
the wind burned their faces and cheeks
and every one of them prayed
for an appointment in the south.   But the storms would not relent
 and the wars went on forever, so a boy called away at sixteen
returned home when he was past 60 to find the fields deserted and overgrown
"She teased me with plumb branches,
   switched me till I bled from the palms, face and shoulders
where the names of her desires are written to this day –
   though she is long beneath the mountain and I'm forced to watch
as most of these memories fade
their shifting figures retreat into the haze like dolls wrapped around machines
   that chatter in the stories I no longer tell.
 So nothing's left to say so I say nothing
   except beg for breakfast and when the girl brings it
I watch her hands attend the tray –
            a soft brown choreography – and I forget
   that I am hungry.
I sit near the window, tray in my lap, and study the approaching light
 as it passes across the pond and the fallen leaves and reaches for my feet
But I am in oblivion, hidden and unformed

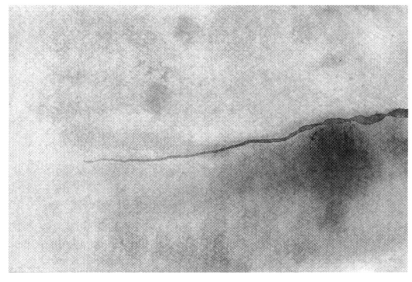

The judges in their silver robes
    have their assignments in purgatory
  to measure light among the speechless cells
  and release strange fruit from the poplar trees
  They walk in circles chanting
  waiting for the day to break wide open
and let the weird light in)

    When he woke up
      he looked out over a vast sea of stones and said,
        "If a sparrow can crush the universe with his song
        why should I fear a man, or a god, or any being?"

I wrestle with dragons
    in the transparent sky
    of nothing mind

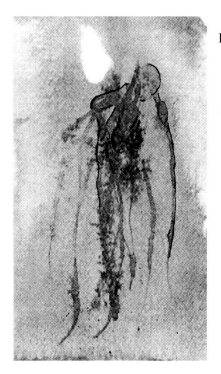

The trunk of the tree
had grown through his spine –
its 12 branches pierced
his chest, arms and legs
He found it impossible to believe
there'd ever been a time
before the orchard
when he moved
freely through the world
Yet, the stories were told.
He overheard them
when the girls came
to harvest the surrounding trees

He heard them sing these old tales
while the sun beat down or the soft
rain fell,
but felt nothing more than the
wound of their singing
or an occasional gesture
(she sat at the table,
hands dancing in the air)
the pleasant sting of salted meat
on the back of his throat
washed to God with the delta soil

"What's the last thing you remember?"

"Dolphins surfacing in shallow water,
   circling a thin pale boy who waved a whale bone cross at the sky.
   I was thinking how soulful her face had become and wondering
if the tiny scars on her back cut like ideograms meant
   anything more than a surgeon's accident."

3.19

"Twelve days out from… traveling north
we came upon another group of priests —
but they knew nothing of the local shrines
or who among the locals might be ill,
and seemed agitated by our inquiries
there was a tension in their voices,
so we did not detain them long.."

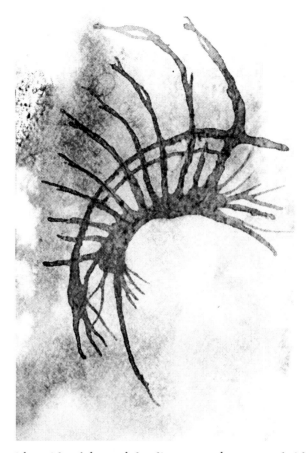

Along either side of the path leading up to the narrow bridge
   villagers had gathered with armloads of black chrysanthemums,
tins of tea and rice, to wish us well in the world beyond ...
2.21   corn stalks in the well –
tar, dust, and river stones in my soup –
The current here carried us swiftly into the gorge, the
   lanterns shattered with their coals still burning as they submerged
  and the streetlights looked like fireflies overhead
   leaving riddles in the rain even the blind carpenter saw.

Through the fog the gulls scattered what remains of the sun,
  garbled radio static took shape in the thick surrounding air,
2.23 half-formed insect prayer beasts snatched fruit from the baskets.
   all night our ears were filled with whispers no one could decipher
  and drinking new wine only intensified their sting.
Come morning we could hear temple bells
  but could see only the sheer cliff face and occasional small tree
  grown from one of the jagged fissures. Out of one of these
   red and yellow moths fluttered in swarms.

An old man mostly down to bone
hangs shirtless from the clouds
   An old claw grips his moon-shaped back as he comes out of the hills
  toward the fields, his horse and plow
The ground's half rock and needs a rain before the seed goes down
  best ask the old woman in the cave for a miracle
She'll pour strong tea into broken pottery
   and hand it across a makeshift pine board table
with wrinkled hands that tremble, but manage to never spill a drop
   She'll ask without looking up how many head,
the shape and color of their horns
   and how often have you seen the crows gather
   in the maple tree that grows beside your front door.
Then she'll stuff her mouth with bitterroot, chew and spit it in her cup
and make sketches of the shapes it makes on a sheet of mulberry leaves,
  walk out leaned upon her cane and tack it to a post wedged between the rocks
   that catches the morning breeze blowing off the southern lakes
She'll ride the clouds for three days after
      and send her answer wrapped in "phoenix wing" for a prayer against fate
  nothing to be done,
   its all blood down river
to summon the sparrow hawk
   before the dry west wind
   blows what's left away,
There's no defense against
the weather's natural claim
   A mouthful of sand and
   broken dishes scattered
      on a hardwood floor,
I'll get back into town
   & two nights with a girl
  who'll do nothing but talk and
   part me from my   money
and say something like,
  "You know of all them country boys
  you're the best one honey."
She'll kiss my forehead, slip on her robe,
   slip quietly away, leaving me lonelier
   than the day before I walked in.
 So now I carry a bag of leaves
   and two white rats in my gut
   as a charm against the Ocean Wife
Who can be seen these early mornings
    in ragged sealskin gowns,
   scrounging the thickets
   for her albino daughter
  and cursing the fading stars

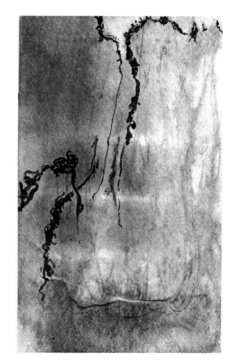

when I look up
  the sky has disappeared

**gates, sacraments,
spells & banishings**

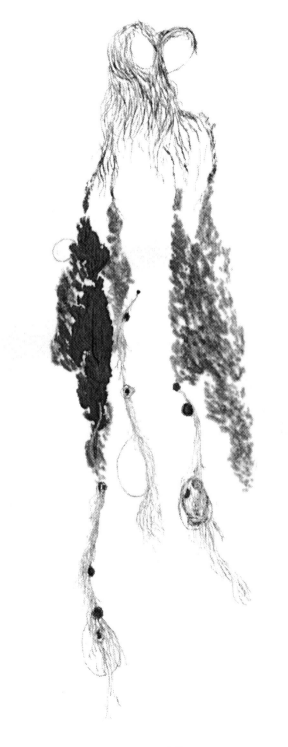

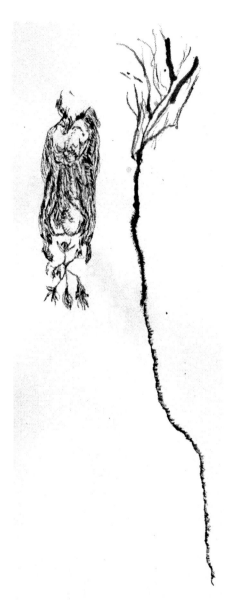

A man who is a swan
   crouched down
  who sang
(dead or alive, can't tell) to
   hustle up the dawn
   and get the
   first day started

When the light came up
the sky laid down screaming
  a blue scarf
  caught in the wind
   I name a seed
    everything
     opening
nucleus mammal hives

  The sun a pulse.

  I am black.

   sky nail

   pollen sac

   Thrones

  a broken branch

  the cedars on fire

   7 faces
   7 wounds

  honey stomach

"In the terrible depths…
They are neither female nor male…
They feed on the gods"

 everything under the sun is on fire
  everything under the sun

I have come here to speak to the dead
 I have come to dissolve them like ashes

 It's a laughter in him
that forces him to break or flower
or break in flowering and die
not lonely, but alone and silent, and
abandon his redemption for nothing sky

everything under the sun is on fire

A man who is a swan
crouched down
who sang (dead creative
can't tell) to
hustle up the dawn
and get the
first day started

When the light came up
the trees laid down, screaming
a blue scarf
caught in the wind
I name a seed
everything
opening
nucleus mammal hides

The sun a pulse.

I am black.

sky road
pollen sac

Thrones
a broken branch
the cedars on fire

7 faces
7 wounds

honey stomach

"In the terrible depths...
They are neither female nor male...
They feed on the gods"

everything under the sun is on fire
everything under the sun

I have come here to speak to the dead
I have come to dissolve them like ashes

It's a laughter in him
that forces him to break or flower
or break in flowering and die
not lonely, but alone and silent,
and abandon his redemption for open sky

everything under the sun is on fire

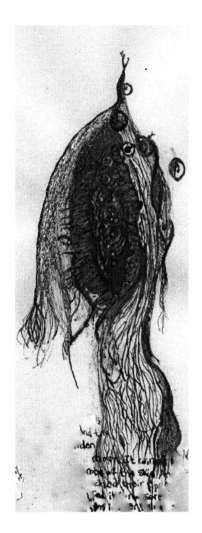

If he extends his thoughts
  toward infinity
they would be scattered by the wind
shattered by the sound
  of night arriving
    So he reaches out
      and they are torn from him –
They drift luminous in the trees

an old philosopher
judged and torn to pieces

(The stammering
    stuttering   pale rain folded –

"I saw him just yesterday,
clear as I am seeing you now.
    And I said, "Where have you been?
    Your eyes
    are like wheels
  As if a machine
      had entered your suffering."

  She was home almost,
    walking,
    long skirts dragging, dirty and wet
"I am always," she paused,
    "I am always returning."
  Her arms outstretched
    her hands
    full of grasping.
"I am always weeping
  when I return from the fields,
but now I feel that
    I have come to the end of it."

   ...not the objects in a night
    but how night knows itself as bare
  blind undreaming tissue –
      layers of skin in hot dissolve

"What did you say just now?"
"I don't know. I was half asleep. Why?"
"I thought you said, 'I am faceted by night.'"

12 days since the beginning of the world
and I have spoken to them in 6.

There was something nearly scandalous in her face. The way her large eyes scanned you emotionlessly and held you – as if behind them lay a room of transgressions. Seething sensual transgressions. A faith. Naked with such clarity it seemed impossible, and mortally dangerous. It made you want her, fear her and despise her all at once.

"Did the thought come? Was it a nice thought? Tell me."
(They are watching a contortionist strip)
The long contours of the muscles in her back when she sat on the bed.

"When the Hittites introduced the horse into warfare it altered even the most fundamental assumptions about civilization. The increase in speed alone gave a calvary a substantial advantage against an army made up entirely of foot soldiers. Add to that the muscular force of horses charging down on men and the increased protection of a chariot. The advantages were short lived however because the Egyptians and Mesopotamians also added the horse to their arsenals. The effect on civilization then was not one of dominance of one culture over another, at least not for long, but a ratcheting up of the force and intensity of warfare."

The walls of this well – its red abyss – I have climbed them for centuries, enamored of their charred surfaces. I have no desire to escape, nor do I enjoy the strenuous climb. Still, as motion is the fundamental compulsion of being, I continue to climb. Insect on a window pane. Circling an inevitable liberation I search myself for the capacity for that extreme moment of cruelty.

"Occasionally, and in some seasons several times a day, I am seized by a feverish pain in my head. The pain is not physical. Nonetheless, it is located inside my skull. I clutch at it with my hands. Sometimes I even strike my head with my fists. Then I am hearing music, somewhere, I don't know – I don't hear it in my ears, it's just there. But as soon as I notice it, it disappears."

His wrists handcuffed behind his back, he wondered how long he'd have to wait before he was discovered.

"Why are you crying?"
"I was thinking about the stillness of ruins; how perfect they are disintegrating. And I wondered how long we would have to wait."

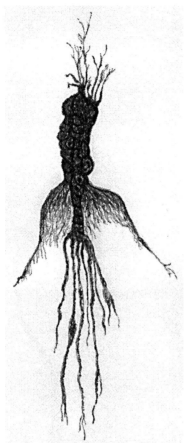

"One can enter that world, but it is forbidden, it has been forbidden for a long time."

"How do you mean forbidden? Who forbids it?"

"No one. It is simply a matter of observation. Everyone here knows that it is forbidden. There are those that come and go through it, but they are like sleepwalkers. They don't realize it. They are only alive in their dreams. Still they are in danger as they pass through. If one of them ever woke he would certainly die."

"So the danger is to go intentionally?"

"No one should ever go, but those that do, and go awake, run the greatest risk. One never altogether returns. Some portion is sacrificed. He is marked. Many who go return destroyed. They usually do not live long. All the same, and you should understand this completely, there is nothing to see and nothing to know. Nothing, precisely. You returned opened forever, carrying an unbearable, impenetrable innocence."

A red-tailed hawk
is bodiless in being hawk –
She is unnamed and undisturbed by names
I read her cry
and disintegrate
soul out lonely snakeskin on railroad tracks —

It is always brown autumn,
and shivering in her long wool coat
tired, heard nothing all day but the
innervating racket of scavenger starlings
and stared across a
red oak table at a gray wall
where it is always autumn
at the corners of our eyes.

In my hand
threads of eternal things.

Driven into the green Mesopotamian hills
  where he fed on lichen and small insects —
  The girls called him Gabriel
    when he came around
    for a bottle of wine
      or a pack of smokes.

  They kept their rifles
    with them in the fields.
  They never knew when
  the winged ancient ones
    might descend.
  The water would be
  cursed and bitter for a month
    and the old women
  could be found
    staring at the shapes it made
  around the rocks in the streams.

      Ocelot

      Raven

    a wild gasoline mare

      Manticore

    Asphodel

        food of the dead:
        bountiful hell.
      All night
        the stillness contaminated
      by thick erotic fevers
          is my engine
      till they kick in the morning door.

How do we fill these empty bodies?
  It is impossible
to make them afraid.
  Some mutation in the cells
the grain is infested with fungus —
  phosphorescent grotesqueries
frescoed across the skull's interior

    but nothing else.
    Not even
    the gracious old fiction
    of memory.

The festivals of the equinox
    lost their character
and slipped into
    dry machine noise
    bronze Baal ghosts
  their eyes turned to light.
A shape in the red clover
  fallen into its genesis
  but there's nothing stranger
  even to themselves
than the fragments of angels
    broken to seed
  in the black loam,
    black Alabama
    black as the hands
    turned it green with blood
to blood fixed in the wood
  and the palms and bare feet
  and the nails nobody told
    hold the shacks together
until electricity releases its worms
      in the frontal lobe
    & sickness makes a stillness &
  in the stillness
      you hear the sickness speak
    a name on fire
      in the seated cloud.
  The long red veil of Ares,
  the astronomers called it,
  stript the river of animal life
      where she reclined
    shrouded in an orchid's flesh,
    stream in a stream,
  back to those chthonic butchers
    who murdered
everything that rises out of the earth
in a white crow's astonishing, empty flight.
    Her hands so tightly wrapped
  around the rose stems
    that her blood ran through her fingers
    redder than the petals
      scattered across the bed –
another sip of tea, another afternoon by the window
  to consider, should I call her father in as second witness
  to these vows performed in red catastrophe
    mouth to mouth
    song to song ——

When you disappeared
your claw
tore at my side, and
stole my breath for most of a week —
and that cool ache in my side
became a companion,
the calm touch of oblivion in my breathing

– 172 –

I caught glimpses of things:

pulp horses

shotgun

chickenwire

cygnus revolver

man in a raincoat

what the humid grass
crucifies

calves foot in
porcelain

night cell
night craw
That black maw of sky
borne
into the well of stars
whose tones
drove the tyrants mad.
The streets buckled and rose

…and the vague birds nesting there
…the second sun

waiting for the mountains to fall,
all blank mind boiling
until your days
are full of the wrenching sound
of flowers opening.

I am listening
to what I know I don't know —
I die
in small pockets of weather
that slap the windows with rain —
or the dragons
gone again
into the clouds.

I wait,
and press my eyelids
until visions come.

What is possible, if anything is possible,
  exists by natural inversions:
  neuron, ganglia, dendrite, synapse,
    a biological paradox of the perverse.
The Invisibles –
    a death in double,
    a double earth.
There are wings in the water.

        Out of the upturned roots
          a man grasps at the sky
          His seizure
        is the nerve of a song
          in tonight's cold wind.
        I pull my collar up beneath my chin
          and walk along
        that nerve's edge
            gathering its poison in a syringe
            that hovers just above the pavement.

        What remains
        I have surrendered to metal,
          out of which
          the mind's green agents
            extract a character
          unknown even to the glands,
            infinite blue,
          and the Real.

    In the dark sockets
  of the doorway unavailable before the tears:
    supernovae
    & sable imaginings flicker
  in cruciform white dogwood
  in a thousand ivory heads
    suspended above the river
  to seed the flood that
      rushes up through the floor boards
  of the house of Cherubim
  taking all
  12 families down

      What lies beyond
        is written in a book
      whose pages are made of lungs
          seamlessly sewn in signatures
        half alive with a green fire
        and written in torturous figures of light —

These letters from Babylon
and the daemon of hours
   Diana, I am writing you,
to explain the circumstances
   of my departure.
   You know already,
how the authorities devised
– with astrolabe and plow,
   microscope and satellite –
a series of criminal events.
   Initially dismissed as art
(obscure choreographies
   and absurd theater),
   the alienists proclaimed the
     incarnation of electro-harmonics
in the person of St. Sigmund —

(a chain of teeth and rubies wrapped in
   brown fur and laid on a bed of tar
set on posts over the body, dead or
       sedated (can't tell).
   As the sun rises the tar begins to melt
   and pour over the body.
By late afternoon it is completely covered.
At twilight a crowd assembles,
   a naked child bearing a torch walks
from among them and
   sets the mass on fire.
The flames rage all night and
   into the next morning.
   The stench is overpowering.
   A blue pall of smoke lingers
in the hollows for days
   until the storms come.

The desert itself is algebra.

There are no cities.

I've seen Gan Eden ripped apart
torn nerve from sinew
    bone from light (word from wind from water)

There is no one always

The house of the Cherubim is charred
    He makes the mountains boil
    He takes even the shadows

    My father is dead
    before he is born
    I am alone in the ur-mirror
    lost in his breathing

He brought her in
    and laid her across the big armchair
  the hem of her dress still tangled with thorns,
    burrs and leaves caught in her hair.
The women keep vigil all night —
(its spring again, the air is warm and close)
    a little ice and rain to ease the fever —
    They keep watch, don't talk much
The room's as vacant as unsexed thought
    unornamented, disenchanted

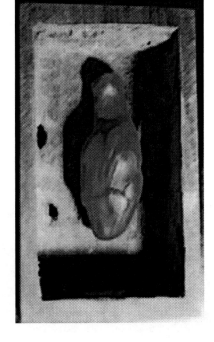

Everything that enters this house
is mistaken for a shadow
Everything that falls
from the overhanging trees
bears the wounding –
describes a sentient echo.

I have taken the chemicals – (mouth to eucharist
in the chemical arts)
(her hands tremble
when she removes the stems
& twists them between
her wrinkled fingertips –
The petals fall for a thousand years)

Everything that stumbles misshapen
out into the rain
has his hands in the reckoning animals.

Everything diminished by
the frailty of arteries and masonry
and the broad ribs spread
knows.

But there is nothing forever
And there are the wings
she folds across her breast.

Dissonance / Seine
for Chris Mansel
now that I have come to the end
and the road's run out into
the same empty sea
that endlessly repeats
in many millioned eyes …
I have burned desire
and come up famished,
utterly hungerless.

The dry seabed
tumbles and rolls
out of habit
out of memory
(though it has no capacities at all)

I have seen the water's creator drown.

with a short length of cord
I murdered the pharmacist
and left his nurse terrified and weeping.
Though I could not see her,
and have imagined her tears.

I am passing you in the darkness?
Can you hear me, am I speaking?
Am I speaking to anyone but myself?
What of all these others?
What of all these empty mouths?
They speak. I see them,
but I am outside their sound.
Their's is a failure of passion —
unreachable, tenacious —
open mouthed, hands struggling for expression.
Their eyes are tender
and savage.
The desert is full of them.
They cry out to raise the serpent,
they crowd the cinemas
and seize the screen with their eyes —
while an incessant chattering den
thickens the air
till air is indistinguishable from earth.
They give it a name: Silence.
and no one hears it.

& I am speaking
  In this movement
    from sand to water
  and the sea is back again
      but only
      as an empty bed
  fallen away
    in the body I renounce
    to discover
    a subtler skin
    made of woven nerve and song.

  "I could feel him surging against me.
  Then suddenly
      he fell still.
    'Is this rape?' I asked myself. I
  barely notice these things anymore."

  They seized the screen with their eyes
    and every one of them vanished.
I walked into an empty theater.
  All they left was the sound of their breathing
  rising and falling in the lightstream.
    Is this rape?
    I barely notice these things anymore.
  I barely notice what the sea has become
    in my waking moments.
    I have skin and veins enough
      even when I don't remember them;
  I have taken the pharmacy for my own
      and dismissed the actors.
  I barely notice
    because the roar in my ears
        is much louder
    than all the phantom shapes
      that rise beyond
      the contentment of murder.

  Down into the river again,
    always,
  that's where it ends;
    into the black water

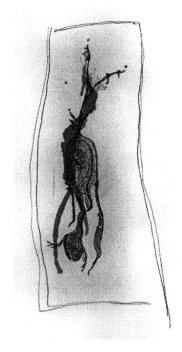

  He sits on the edge of his chair
    fiddling with a cigarette,
    "I can't wait any longer. What
    else can I do?

No. I don't mean for you to answer.
... I can't wait."
He is poised as if he is listening
to a distant cry
from the world to come
or the grinding of wheels
or ditches of bodies.

"But I have no future,"
he says beneath his breath.
"The future went out
like a lamp while I waited.
Now I enter the pharmacy alone
and take the life I've been given
and delete my drugged disappearance."

He was under the bridge.
and I crouched in the window
and watched
while he scattered bottles
of colored elixir into the water,
and the women in shrouds
walked single file
to the hill where the bodies were laid.
And the crows fed.
alone, alone, alone.
each of them alone,
tore at the sheets.

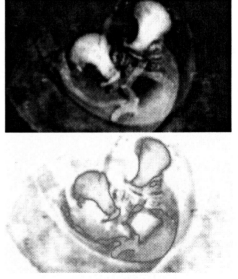

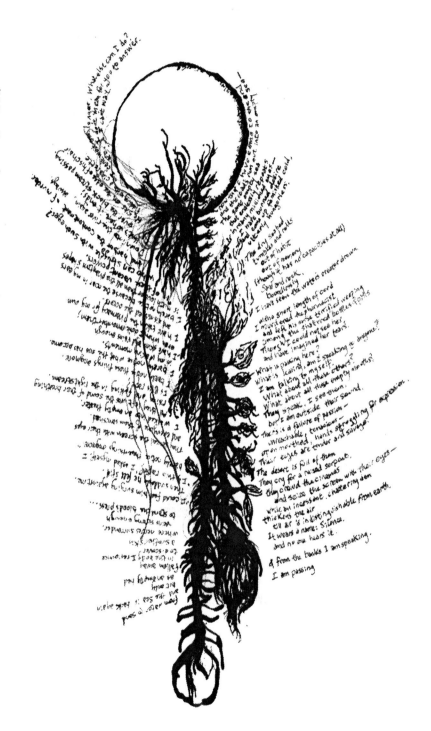

Heraclitus realized the primacy of fire. It's nature is paradox – a frictional tension that ignites the human brain. We speak. At first sounds only – we do not know what we are saying. But a secondary fire, child of the first, and its mirror, rises out of the darkness beyond sound. The fire, in this sense, knows itself – and then recognizes its fallen nature. It is neither sound or silence. It seeks redemption and understands itself as alone, as a wanderer in the wilderness. Out of grace the original fire seeks the annihilation of the second. Nietzsche, like St. John of the Cross, knew that the night, too, is a sun. Everything falls away. Chaos is warm. Chaos is a motherfigure.

I hear animal shapes in the song
    I know by these blasphemies I have eaten the gods
        in disturbed electron clouds –
    Chaos tastes of musk and glittering
        in some other brain.
        Follow it out:
        The house sparrows
        rustling in the eaves
            just before dawn

    I am awake
in a grave-digger's face.
    Light gathers in the leaves,
        spills off the branches
and destroys his morning's work.

    I crave the white crow's scar and voice.
His flight
    is full of spells and banishings.

        Rosa Mundi
        Rose of the World
        where the eye is a swarm of flies
            in the swarm's blue voice

"Don't move," she said, "don't breathe."
"You must learn to stop breathing."

These mysteries
 are the color
of the doves that nest in the cypress
 and startle out
when I throw the window open.

 These sacraments:
  The swan.
  The crow.
    The mare in the corn.
   The horse I have ridden to death
    in this field
     where Memory is destroyed.

 These sacraments
  are the tales the old people told
 around the evening table –
  Their hands waving around wildly
 to draw the pictures out
    along the story's length.
   They are full of spells and banishings
   and the deep earth
     vanishing out of their mouths.

These sacraments:
 A child's arm is severed
and fed to the populace.
 She bends down in the field,
lifts a large clay pot toward heaven,
  places it on her shoulder and walks away.
Prayers in the threshing house.
  She was 15 when the armies came
  and killed all the men.

 These sacraments:
 They are planting the testicles
of her dead lover.
  He beat the rock with his fists
until his fingers were broken and bleeding.
   In the streets
    they called him "laughing boy"
    even when he was old, derelict
    and never smiled
    and no one remembered why.

These are the sacraments:
   There is a place in heaven
      for men who design land mines.
   There is a place in hell
      for the innocent bodies
   they destroy.

   These gates:
      Chaos is warm.
      In the dance
   her belly is an exaggerated face.
      Her vulva is a grotesque smile.
   Everyone laughs.

Along the corridor
   underground
   beneath the heaving bridges
They tore her father's herd to pieces
   and nailed them to the barricades.
   Everyone laughed.
      Nine months later
      they buried the bones
         beneath the crying tree.

   I was a child.
      I was sick most of the time.
   My mother told me
      about the wreck of cinema
in old America.
      Everything changed after that.

   These sacraments:
      Information sickness
   and the plunder of Yggdrasil.

7 robes laid across the bed
   like 7 skins –
one for each lover
   he kept in a closet behind the wall.
   The lemons and peaches on
   the window sill
      with a green light falling.
"The weather is close,"
   he whispered to No One
   rocking side to side,
      "storms are coming."

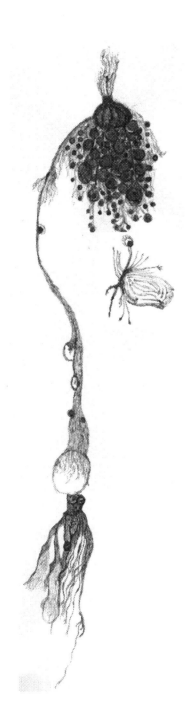

The cicada's song
　　　steady and dry. Insect metal
　　drumming up the heat –
　　They are chanting
　　in a hospital corridor, in
　　the waiting rooms,
　　in the family of the dead
　　waiting for word,
　in the nurse coming toward you
　　　in a cruel clinical light.

　　　Chaos is warm.
　　These sacraments:
(I don't want to talk to you anymore.)
　　She opens her mouth
　　to say – I'm sorry –
　　but all you can see
　　are the gods in her eyes
　　and the room wheels and drops
　　and the lights go out.
　　I fell to my knees
　　and cried out to No One:
　"I'm tore open raw and clean,
　I got a heart like railroad steel.
　I'm tore open raw and clean,
I got a heart as hard as railroad steel.
I'm going down to the slaughterhouse
and find me something young to kill."

　　　A voice said to me,
　"The cave that you have forgotten,
and all those generations before you,
　contains an underground stream.
　　It's water is warm and
　　a fog rises out of the cave
and calls the water bearers in."
　　They return
　　with vessels on their shoulders.

　　These are the sacraments.
　　There are no cities.
　　Chaos is warm.

Businessmen devoured the cities
  and flew around Europe, Asia,
  & Africa
    covered in soldiers –
birth, war and violent expenditure –
  The dissolute sigh
    in sex
    in death
  The thick electric cable
    that runs through my vertebrae
  and explodes across my chest.
  So much of this agitation
    is just the Neural Wave singing –
  gone, gone, always gone
      into the dirt or air.

In the north,
    in a thick fog,
The Neural Wave breaks up in static –
    you hear fragments –
  you remember your body in pieces
    though you do not remember it as your own.
    A hand
    A ring
      a lullaby your mother sang,
      a face in the mirror
        you can't explain.

  I was sick
    and wet with fever –
  Now I am sick again
    and I speak
  out of that wet distance.
  My voice is thick and heavy –
  The sea
    makes shapes in the cloud.

  I came here
    to speak to the dead
  and found them alive
      and possessed by a green fire –
branches and leaves
grew from their shoulders…

At the confluence of these rivers
       our voices mingle –
 our forms are inseparable.
       We move through one another.
 We drink wilderness.

             Here, in this place,
       The mirrors explode
             The windows are electric alive
 I fold my hands on my lap and study
       the raw nerve trees burning
       I move in their fever
 Here, with these others,
       I am a gesture

 out of that wet distance –
       out of that

AUTHOR'S NOTES

It is impossible to know which words and phrases to include in a series of notes to a poem. What I have tried to include here are those things that might be difficult to find in an ordinary dictionary or encyclopedia. However, with a resource like the internet increasingly at hand, most of what I include here could easily be traced if one wished to do so. But I have tried to include some of the more obscure terms, and more importantly, terms drawn from personal experience. However, there are many words that are inventions, either by glossolalia (ecstatic utterance), or inventions of words from root origins. These terms are intentionally left undefined and open for the reader to discover, on a personal level, their content and meaning.

Additionally, my use of the words from various myths, religions, symbolisms, and sciences is not intended as an act of appropriation for my own purposes. That would go against the very nature of what *Brambu Drezi* is, a completely open work, without boundaries. These words should be taken for their conventional meaning, and that meaning should be incorporated into the understanding of the work. That is, I do not use them to explain my personal experience, but to generate an experience that is beyond me, and as mysterious to me as anyone who reads or hears the work.

BOOK ONE

11) Myelacephalon—according to *Mosby's Medical And Nursing Dictionary*, myelacephalus is defined as "a fetal monster, usually a separate monozygotic twin, whose form and parts are barely recognizable; a slightly differentiated amorphous mass."

11) "legion swollen faces"—When I was ten years old I began to suffer intense hypnogogic attacks. Upon waking I would require as much as an hour to recover. The substance of these attacks consisted of seeing disembodied swollen heads drifting and swooning down on me. When I woke I felt completely isolated from my environment, actuated by the sensation that my skin was spongy and tingly, as if being pricked by hundreds of tiny needles.

13) Facing The Leopard—this phrase comes from a dream in which a friend and I took a boat down a stream into the underworld. We came upon a cabin perched on a high bank. We climbed a rope ladder to get inside where there was an informal gathering of some sort. There I met a man who was understood to be the master of the house and who looked exactly like Michael McClure, with longish gray hair. At this point I had not met him personally, nor had any contact with him, knowing him only through his books. In the photographs on the back of all his books at the time his hair appeared to be very dark. In the dream I asked him, "how do I climb higher?" He answered, "first, you must face the leopard."

15) ABRAXAS —An ancient deity of uncertain origin, often associated with the 365 days of the solar year. Certain gnostic sects in the early centuries CE appear to have worshipped ABRAXAS in some form. The term abracadabra probably shares with it a common origin.

15) Bardo—according to the *Tibetan Book of the Dead,* any realm of sentient beings, but specifically the abode of the dead.

15) Shekinah—in Jewish mysticism, the abiding presence of God in the Holy of Holies, or in the community generally. According to some scholars and mystics Shekinah is a feminine aspect of God.

16) Jachin's pillar—one of the pillars on either side of the High Priestess in the Tarot.

17) hermit in Waukau—the artist Malok, who lives in Waukau, Wisconsin, with whom I have corresponded for twenty years.

17) slept in a cave for 13 years with his son—from Jewish legend. Rabbi Akiba ben Joseph is said to have lived in a cave for 13 years. He is the writer, according to tradition, of the Sepher Yitzirah, or Book of Formation, the earliest written text of Kabbalah.

24) wool of Mithras—a reference to the cult of Mithras, a solar, messianic deity prevalent in the Middle East around the time of Christ. The commonality of symbolism and legend between the two religions is significant.

25) dedicated to wZ the musician, artist, and traveler, a long-time companion and kindred spirit, a brother. The phrase "an energy that surpasses reality" is a quote from one of his letters.

30) "the faire White Woman married to the Ruddy Man"—quoting an alchemical text, probably one referenced in C. G. Jung's *Mysterium Coniunctionis,* which I was reading at the time (c. 1987).

41) Merkabah—the chariot of God as seen in Ezekiel's vision. It continues to precipitate much speculation.

41) Kali—the dark aspect of the goddess in Hindu mythology.

41) loa—the pantheon of saints in the Vodoun religion of Haiti.

49) "Emergent Seas" was inspired by a work of sculpture given to me by the artist Mimi Holmes.

52) Ein Soph—a term used to describe the reality of God beyond what is knowable. It originates in Jewish mysticism.

52) Adam Kadmon—the primordial man, the archetype if you will, of the human creature.

52) histanai—Greek, literally "out from standing," or that which presents itself to the senses, i.e. has being. From my reading of Heidegger, especially *An Introduction to Metaphysics*.

58) Rattlesnake Disc—written for my brother Jon, who gave me a replica of the stone "rattlesnake disc" that was discovered at Moundville, the pre-Columbian city just south of what is now Tuscaloosa, Alabama. The inhabitants of Moundville were of the Mississippian culture that flourished in the southeastern region of today's United States from roughly 900-1500 CE. The symbolism closely resembles the Mesoamerican cultures of the same period.

62) Chenrazi and Avalokita—two different versions of the Buddha of compassion, from Tibetan and Indian mythology respectively.

62) Uktena—a legendary monster among the Cherokee peoples of the American Southeast. It had qualities of both a fish and a bird.

63) the graph-like glyphs that appear on this page were generated by equations taken from Chaos theory.

66) out it blows—a literal translation of the word nirvana.

BOOK TWO

1) "UMGATHAMA"—The word arrived as a result of hypnogogic vision. As I lay on my bed one evening Charles Olson stood over me repeating the word "UMGATHAMA" with great force, but not anger. The urgency in his voice suggested he was bringing a message from a poetic realm. It was therefore a word of power, an address of the holy, which is how it continues to arise throughout *Brambu Drezi*. I was surprised that Olson should be the messenger since I had read only small portions of his work, and was particularly impressed by "In Cold Hell, In Thicket." Since then I have read *The Maximus Poems*, various other poems and essays, as well as Tom Clark's biography of Olson, *The Allegory of a Poet's Life*. I subsequently developed a better sense of why it was Olson who appeared to me.

75) "Thomas Rhymer"—Thomas The Rhymer, Thomas of Erdedoune, lived during the 13th century in Scotland, a seer and political figure contemporary with Robert the Bruce and William Wallace. According to old ballads he gained vision or prophetic insight as the result of his relationship with the Fairy Queen. The minister Robert Kirk is very important in this connection, primarily for his book *The Secret Commonwealth of Elves, Fauns, and Fairies*.

75) "7 red hot stones"—the stones used in Sioux sweatlodge ceremonies.

76) "langage"—the sacred language used in Voudoun ceremonies, the "Brambu" as a qualifier here, meaning the sacred tongue (or part of it) of this particular body of work.

76) "Nova Cygni 1992"—a nova in the constellation Cygnus (the swan). Cygnus is important in mythology, but also here because it is the "house" of a peculiar x-ray source that is now generally accepted to be a black hole. The incredible gravity of black holes makes them primary "dislocators" in the universe, an interjection of chaos. Also, as they are impossibly dense and dark, one thinks of the dark, hellish fires in Boehme, Blake, Gnosticism, and Hebrew mysticism. It could be said that the swan bears in her body a dark attractor beyond whose "event horizon" nothing can be known.

77) "paths of the dragon" (lung mei)—Chinese concept of earth force carried in the ground. Two categories: yin = white tiger (female) and yang = azure dragon (male).

77) "to gather paradise"—quoting Emily Dickinson.

78) "How do we speak to one another?" This line was unconsciously "borrowed" from Jack Foley. I wasn't aware that I had taken it from him until we performed together at Cody's Books in Oakland, CA in April,1996. I read an excerpt from Brambu Drezi that included the borrowed line. Jack followed, performing multi-voiced poems with his wife Adelle. We had not spoken prior to the reading about what either of us was planning to perform, but Jack and Adelle performed his "Chorus: King Amour," which included the lines:

> how can we
> "speak"
> to one another –
> what is
> "between" us –
> (words
> or
> looks?)

I was shocked to realize that I'd taken the line from Jack. I promised myself that when the book was published I would give credit where it was due.

79) "Bondeye"—the supreme head of the pantheon of loa in Voudoun, the creator spirit. A similar figure exists in East African religions. It is said that one can see only his footprints, therefore Bondeye is beyond all things. As such, I associate the deity with the Kabbalist's Ein Soph.

80) "Catal Hüyük"—The account of the use of chemicals at Catal Hüyük is of my own devising. In fact very little is known about the ancient site with any degree of certainty. There have been speculations of goddess worship, a vulture cult, and a goddess associated with a leopard (which connects it with Brambu Drezi).

81) "mi" (who?), "mah"(what?)—means of creation by Ein-Soph according to the prologue of the Zohar.

81)"Ptah"—Egyptian creator god. Translated, the name means "opener," connecting it to the first line of Book Two. Similar is the Hebrew Petah 'Enaim, translated as "eye opener."

81) "Cetus-Algol"—Cetus is a constellation, and in Greek mythos a sea monster. Algol is Arabic, translated as "the ghoul," a demon, and an eclipsing binary star in Perseus.81) "M81-82"—two interactive galaxies that, seen in Hydrogen-Alpha light, display massive dust clouds and an eye-like halo.

82) "áshe"—from Santeria, loosely translated as "the life force" of all things, including the divine forces.

83) "cochiery"—word spoken to me by Sun Ra, the late jazz composer/performer, in a dream. It was to be my new name he said. I was unable to understand what he said at first, and had to go back to sleep and into the dream to ask him to repeat it. The word I have used is as close an approximation as I was able to bring back.

83) "Arsiel"—from Hebrew, translated as "black sun." See note to "Nova Cygni" above.

84) "Loko"—sacred fire in the Fon religion of East Africa.

87) "Malkisedheq" or Melchizidek—Hebrew, an ancient priest king of Jerusalem. According to Hebrew and Christian tradition this is also an order of priesthood that has no beginning or end.

87) "valences"—valence band or the range of highest possible energies an electron can have and still be associated with a particular atom to form bonds; the power field.

95) "Neter-Khertet"—ancient Egyptian common name for the abode of the dead; it translates as the "divine subterranean place."

96) "Padma"—Padma Sambhava, legendary figure who brought Tantric Buddhism to Tibet.

98) "Adhira"—Sanskrit, "she who is blissfully unstable in loving excitement."

99) "Black Hand"—an evil guardian knight of the grail castle until Perceval defeated him.

104) "fraylings"—term used by the Norse in North America to describe the natives.

104) "KTR" and "MLKT"—transliterations from the Hebrew of Kether (Crown) and Malkuth (Kingdom), the highest and lowest sephiroth on the kabbalistic tree of life.

104) "Ap-uat"—ancient Egyptian, "opener of ways."

105) "Opal"—hurricane Opal, 1995.108) "thyroid storm"—defined in *Mosby's Medical & Nursing Dictionary* as a "crisis in uncontrolled hyperthyroidism caused by a release in the blood stream of increased amounts of thyroid hormones. Characteristic signs are fever that may reach 106° F., a rapid pulse, acute respiratory distress, apprehension, restlessness, irritability, and prostration. The patient may become delirious, lapse into a coma and die of heart failure."

109) Molly Durga—the Goddess who drove the demons from India.

109) "Katoptron"—Greek, mirror used to focus light, literally "going to see."

109) "Wüd,"—Scottish alternate of Old English "wood," meaning mad, insane.

110) "Chac"—Mayan rain deity, Chac-Xib. Venus as new evening star.

112) "How does one name the holy?"—quoting the first line of Jack Foley's "Requiem."

114) "telesorium"or telesensorium—to send and/or receive an entire sensory field.

115) "Eleleth"—according to an ancient gnostic text, "The Hypostasis of the Archons," a great angel who reveals how the world of matter came into being.

118) "Herü"or Horus—the ancient Egyptian deity, son of Osiris and Isis, represented sometimes as a hawk. The figure on this page is a tracing of an imprint a hawk left on our kitchen window after crashing into it.

118) "gone to earth"—a phrase used in fox hunting indicating that the fox has gone into a hole in the ground.

120) "Abulafia"—Abraham Abulafia, 13th century mystic, ecstatic kabbalist.

122) "El-Aima"—a figure of the goddess using Hebrew terms for deity in the feminine.

BOOK THREE

132) "here we go…"—quoting Mircea Costache, Romanian shepherd, as translated in *National Geographic*, Vol. 194, No. 3, Sept 1998.

138) Marah —the great sea, kabbalistic correspondence to the third sephiroth Binah, "intelligence."141) "Three days into the mountains…" —based on the account of the fate of a paternal ancestor as told by my father.

147) "the jade fungus of immortality"—quoting from Lu Yu, "The Old Man That Does As He Pleases," in his *Diary Of A Trip To Shu*, referring to Taoist alchemy.

148) all the spiraling events—all the obvious: galaxies, DNA, but also Yeats' ideas of time and event, the gyre.

152) "The factories bombed …"—This quote is based on a conversation with my paternal grandfather about his experiences in the Pacific as a sailor in World War II.

154) "They say there is…"—excerpted from an anonymously written poem from the ancient anthology of Japanese poetry Kokinshu *(Collection of Ancient and Modern Times)*, completed around 920 CE.

155) "How long can a reflection or a shadow last?"—Han-shan Te-ching (1546-1623).

156) komuso—translates from the Japanese as "priest of nothingness (or emptiness)." They wandered the countryside, cities and towns, begging their living and performing various prayers and healing rituals. They practiced "sui-zen," that is, playing the shakuhachi bamboo flute as a prerequisite to, or perhaps in lieu of, sitting meditation. They used the flute in their healing rituals as well. Komuso were also distinguished by their large basket-like woven hats, which covered their faces entirely, making them anonymous and discouraging individual pride in meritorious deeds. Unfortunately, according to some accounts government spies and displaced samurai (ronin) also donned the attire of the komuso for their own purposes.

168) "In the terrible depths…"—from an Akkadian hymn/spell (c. 2000 B.C.). Borrowed from "The Seven," translated by Jerome Rothenberg in *Technicians of the Sacred: A Range of Poetics from Africa, America, Asia, and Oceania.*

171) "Did the thought..."—from *La Notte,* a film directed by Michaelangelo Antononi.

173) "Driven into..."—thinking of the Biblical account of Nebuchadnezzar.

180) "Dissonance/Seine"—partially drawn from the events of the life of Paul Celan.

182) The last lines of "Dissonance/ Seine"are an image of Zoroastrian burial practices.

185) "They are planting ... "—taken from various accounts of the rites of Attis and Adonis.

Breinigsville, PA USA
14 September 2009

224072BV00004B/1/A